CONTENT

MW00908385

**Suggested use
for the week of:**

Bible Study at a Glance

Start here

Leader Bible Study

Familiarize yourself with the context of the Bible story and how it relates to God's plan of redemption.

Session Starters

Activity Page

Small Group Opening

Use opening activities and session starters to introduce the day's Bible story.

Say what?
Use the suggested "Leader" and "Say" dialogue to easily move between segments.

Key Passage

Timeline Map

Big Picture Question

Large Group Leader

This 30-minute teaching time allows you to watch or tell the Bible story. Large group elements reinforce the Bible story and Christ Connection.

Review

Sing

The Gospel: God's Plan for Me

Discussion Starter

Suggested times
The times provided allow you to complete the session plan in an hour and fifteen minutes. Lengthen or shorten the session as needed.

Make it fit

Customize the session plan to fit the needs of your church or classroom.

 1 room

1) Use the Small Group Opening to welcome kids to Bible Study. Kids may work the activity page and/or complete an activity together.
2) Transition to an area within your classroom that can be designated as the Large Group Bible story area. Watch the Bible story video or tell the Bible story. Incorporate any large group elements that fit your space and your time constraints.
3) Regroup to the Small Group area by using a countdown video or gather around a table as you review the key passage and practice Bible skills.

 1 or more rooms

1) Use the Small Group Opening to welcome kids to Bible Study. Kids may work the activity page and/or complete an activity together.
2) Use the countdown video or other transition signal as you move your small group to join the other small groups in the Large Group area. Watch the Bible story video or tell the Bible story. Incorporate any large group elements that fit your space and your time constraints.
3) Regroup to the Small Group rooms where you will reinforce what the kids learned from

Key Passage Activity

Journal

Bible Story Review & Bible Skills

Small Group Leader

Review the Bible story, build Bible skills, engage in activity options, and more!

Activities

Check out our tips and resources for an additional hour in the Worship Guide!

Finish here

Unit 34: THE EARLY CHURCH

Big Picture Questions

Session 1:
By whose power did Peter heal the man who was lame? Peter healed the man by the power of Jesus.

Session 2:
Who can do God's work? God gives every believer skills for doing His work.

Session 3:
Why was Stephen not afraid to die? Stephen saw Jesus waiting for him in heaven.

Unit 34: THE EARLY CHURCH

Unit Description: The gospel is good news for everyone, both Jews and Gentiles. Through the early church, the good news about Jesus spread beyond Jerusalem. The Lord saved more and more people every day, and the church grew.

Unit Key Passage:
Acts 2:42,47

Unit Christ Connection:
The church is God's plan to bring praise and glory to Jesus.

Session 1:
The Church Met Needs
Acts 3:1-10; 4:32-37

Session 2:
Seven Men Were Chosen
Acts 6:1-7

Session 3:
Stephen's Address
Acts 6:8–7:60

Leader BIBLE STUDY

The lives of Jesus' disciples had been virtually turned upside-down. In a short matter of time, their Lord Jesus had been crucified and then raised from the dead. He appeared to many people, commissioned His disciples to take the gospel into the world, and ascended to heaven before their eyes.

After the Holy Spirit came and the disciples began preaching the gospel, more and more people believed in Jesus. They met together and shared what they had. God blessed them, and the church grew. (See Acts 2.)

Peter and John were among Jesus' first disciples. They were fishermen, and when Jesus called them, Peter and John immediately left their work and followed Him. (Matt. 4:18-22) Peter and John still followed Christ after His ascension. Though Jesus was no longer with them physically, the Holy Spirit empowered them to do God's work.

One day, Peter and John encountered a man at the temple gate. The man was lame, and he depended on the generosity of passersby. When the man looked at Peter and John, he likely hoped for or expected money. Gold or silver would have provided food or clothing, but Peter gave him something even more valuable.

"In the name of Jesus Christ the Nazarene, get up and walk!" (Acts 3:6) Peter reached out and helped the man to his feet. He was healed! Not by Peter's power, but by the power of Jesus working through him.

God was working through the early church. His grace changed people's hearts so they would believe in Jesus. They lived in a way that didn't make sense to the world—sharing what they had so no one was needy. The same Holy Spirit that worked among believers then is with believers today. By His power the church can tell others about Jesus and show them His love.

Older Kids BIBLE STUDY OVERVIEW

Session Title: The Church Met Needs
Bible Passage: Acts 3:1-10; 4:32-37
Big Picture Question: By whose power did Peter heal the man who was lame? Peter healed the man by the power of Jesus.
Key Passage: Acts 2:42,47
Unit Christ Connection: The church is God's plan to bring praise and glory to Jesus.

Small Group Opening

Large Group Leader

Small Group Leader

Additional suggestions for specific groups are available at *gospelproject.com/kids/additional-resources*.

For free online training on how to lead a group, visit *ministrygrid.com/web/thegospelproject*.

The BIBLE STORY

The Church Met Needs
Acts 3:1-10; 4:32-37

One afternoon, Peter and John—two of Jesus' followers—**went to the temple**. It was time **to pray.** When they got there, **Peter and John saw a man sitting by a gate. The man could not walk,** so he could not work. Every day, the man's friends carried him to the temple, where **he sat outside. The gate** was called the Beautiful Gate. As people entered the temple, they walked by the man, and the man asked them for money.

Peter said to the man, "Look at us." The man looked at Peter and John, expecting to receive something from them.

Peter said, "I don't have any silver or gold for you, but I will give you what I do have." Then Peter said, "In the name of Jesus Christ of Nazareth, get up and walk!"

Peter reached out and helped the man up. All of a sudden, the man's feet and ankles were strong. He could walk! In fact, the man leaped around! **He went into the temple with Peter and John, and he praised God.**

The people in the temple saw the man. Wasn't this the man who sat by the gate outside the temple every day? The man who asked for money because he couldn't walk? Yes, it was the man! And he was healed! How could such a wonderful thing happen? **The people were amazed at what they saw.**

Now all the people who believed in Jesus got along as if they were all part of the same family. No one kept anything just for themselves. **They shared everything they had.** Jesus' followers told people about Jesus' resurrection. "Jesus is alive!" they said. **And God was kind to them.** No one in the group needed anything because if anyone in the church owned land or houses, they sold what they had and gave the money to Jesus' disciples. Then **the disciples made sure everyone was taken care of.**

Christ Connection: After Jesus returned to heaven, the Holy Spirit gave the disciples power to keep working. Peter healed a man who was lame with the power of Jesus' name. God changed the hearts of believers, and they shared what they had so no one was needy. God gives the Holy Spirit to believers today so the church can tell others about Jesus and show them His love.

Want to discover God's Word? Get *Bible Express*!

Invite kids to check out today's devotional to discover that, just as Jesus sent the Holy Spirit to be with the early church, God promised Joshua that He would be with him. (Joshua 1:5) God will never leave us, and He will help us accomplish the job He has for us! Order in bulk, subscribe quarterly, or purchase individually. For more information, check out *www.lifeway.com/devotionals*.

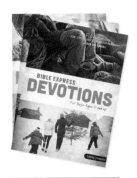

The Early Church

Small Group OPENING

Session Title: The Church Met Needs
Bible Passage: Acts 3:1-10; 4:32-37
Big Picture Question: By whose power did Peter heal the man who was lame? Peter healed the man by the power of Jesus.
Key Passage: Acts 2:42,47
Unit Christ Connection: The church is God's plan to bring praise and glory to Jesus.

Welcome time

Greet each kid as he or she arrives. Use this time to collect the offering, fill out attendance sheets, and help new kids connect to your group. Ask kids to talk about a time this week that they helped someone else. Kids may also share about a time someone else helped them.

Activity page (5 minutes)

- "Story Words Mix-Up" activity page, 1 per kid
- pencils

Invite kids to work individually or in pairs to complete the "Story Words Mix-Up" activity page. Kids will unscramble the words related to today's Bible story. When kids finish, review the answers together. (*church, needs, heal, share, Peter, power*)

Say • Does anyone know what these words have in common? They all are in the Bible story we are going to hear today. The story is about Peter, the church, and … well, you'll soon find out!

Session starter (10 minutes)

Option 1: Get moving
Invite kids to spread out around the room. Choose a volunteer to be the leader at the front of the room. Explain

that the leader will do one of three things: clap, cheer, or stomp. Designate a response for each leader action:

- Clap: walk in place
- Cheer: skip around the room
- Stomp: jump up and down

Encourage the leader to do several actions and challenge kids to respond with the corresponding motion. Allow a few volunteers a turn to be the leader.

Say • In today's Bible story, someone who had been unable to use his legs was suddenly able to walk and leap around! Praise God!

Option 2: Middle name introductions

Guide boys and girls to sit in a circle. Instruct one player to begin by introducing herself by her middle name: "Hi, I'm Grace." The next player should introduce himself, as well as the previous player: "I'm James, and this is Grace."

Continue around the circle. Each player should introduce himself and every player before him to help kids learn the names. When everyone has been introduced, challenge kids to play a name game. Explain that one kid will begin by saying his middle name and then the middle name of any other player in the circle. That player will say her middle name and then another player's middle name.

Play will move from kid to kid as they learn each other's middle names.

Say • Did you know that the Bible says there is a name that is powerful and greater than every name? (Jer. 10:6; Phil. 2:9) Today we are going to hear about a man who healed a man with the power of Jesus' name.

Transition to large group

Large Group LEADER

Session Title: The Church Met Needs
Bible Passage: Acts 3:1-10; 4:32-37
Big Picture Question: By whose power did Peter heal the man who was lame? Peter healed the man by the power of Jesus.
Key Passage: Acts 2:42,47
Unit Christ Connection: The church is God's plan to bring praise and glory to Jesus.

• room decorations

Tip: Select decorations that fit your ministry and budget.

Suggested Theme Decorating Ideas: Simulate a tree house under construction by hanging a picture of a large tree on a focal wall. Position various building supplies and tools at the front of the room. Consider displaying a ladder, some scrap pieces of sanded wood, tape measures, blueprints, safety glasses, and a toolbox. You might rope off a section of the large group area with caution tape.

Countdown

• countdown video

Show the countdown video as your kids arrive, and set it to end as large group time begins.

Introduce the session (3 minutes)

• leader attire
• safety glasses
• large sheet of paper
• pencil

[Large Group Leader enters wearing safety glasses. A pencil is tucked behind his or her ear, and he or she is carefully studying a sheet of paper.]

Leader • I'm just not sure this is going to work! If we put the rope bridge on this side of the window, there might not be enough room for the secret hatch!

   [Look up to see kids.] Hi! Do any of you have any experience building a tree house? I want to build one with my dad in my backyard, but first I have to decide on a

design. There are just so many cool features you can put in a tree house these days: bay windows, rope ladders, rope swings, rope bridges, bunk beds, secret hatches, balconies … What kind of things would you include on a tree house? [*Allow kids to respond.*]

[*Roll up the paper.*] Those are all great ideas, but that's probably enough for now. I'm starting to feel overwhelmed! I think designing and building the perfect tree house would be nothing short of a miracle! Speaking of miracles, I want you to hear today's Bible story! Are you ready? Let's check it out.

Timeline map (2 minutes)

• Timeline Map

Leader • Here is our timeline map. It helps us see the big picture of God's story in the Bible—from the time the world began all the way to … here! [*Point to today's Bible story picture.*]

This is where we will start today, "The Church Met Needs." At this point in the big story, Jesus had returned to heaven and His disciples were telling others the good news about Jesus, how He died on the cross for our sins and rose again. The believers—those who trusted in Jesus—met together. They made up the church, and the church was growing. You could say God was building the church. I don't mean the physical church *building*, but every day more and more people believed in Jesus, so the church grew.

Now, here's a picture of a guy sitting on a mat. He looks kind of weak and sad. But these two other guys look strong and happy. This is Peter and John. They were two of Jesus' followers, and they were going to the temple to pray. I wonder if they helped this man.

Big picture question (1 minute)

Leader • That's what we are going to find out when we answer our big picture question. When you listen to the Bible story, see if you can figure out the answer. *By whose power did Peter heal the man who was lame?* Oh, boy. It sounds like Peter, one of these strong-looking men, did help the man. The man was lame. That means he wasn't able to use his legs.

Tell the Bible story (10 minutes)

• "The Church Met Needs" video
• Bibles, 1 per kid
• Bible Story Picture Slide or Poster
• Big Picture Question Slide or Poster

Tip: A Bible story script is provided at the beginning of every session. You may use it to guide you as you prepare to teach the Bible story in your own words. For a shorter version of the Bible story, read only the bolded text.

Open your Bible to Acts 3 and tell the Bible story in your own words, or show the Bible story video "The Church Met Needs."

Leader • Wow! All of this happened after Jesus died on the cross, rose from the dead, and ascended to heaven. The people who followed Jesus had a job to do—to tell others about Him! Peter and John were part of the group of believers who made up the early church.

The Bible says the man at the temple gate had been lame since birth. His life must have been difficult. We know that he could not work. He sat at the temple gate and begged for money, probably so he could buy food.

When Peter and John stopped to talk to the man, he must have thought they were going to give him money. But then Peter told him that he didn't have any silver or gold. Instead, Peter gave the man something even better— healing! Peter healed the man, but not by his own power. *By whose power did Peter heal the man who was lame? Peter healed the man by the power of Jesus.*

The Bible says that Peter healed the man "in the name of Jesus." That means that Jesus worked through Peter. When Peter said that he healed the man by the power of Jesus, he meant that Peter was not the one healing the man; Jesus was working through Peter. ***By whose power did Peter heal the man who was lame? Peter healed the man by the power of Jesus.***

Peter and John were part of the early church. We learned that they prayed, and sometimes Jesus used them to do miracles. What else did the early believers do? How did they live?

Our Bible story tells us that they lived as though they were all part of the same family. They shared what they had, and most importantly, they told people about Jesus. They told people that He is alive! By hearing this good news—the gospel—and believing it, people are saved from their sin.

The Gospel: God's Plan for Me (optional)

Using Scripture and the guide provided, explain to boys and girls how to become a Christian. Tell kids how they can respond, and provide counselors to speak with each kid individually. Guide counselors to use open-ended questions to allow kids to determine the direction of the conversation.

Encourage boys and girls to ask their parents, small group leaders, or other adults any questions they may have about becoming a Christian.

Key passage (4 minutes)

• Key Passage Slide or Poster
• "Every Day" song

Display the key passage poster and read it aloud. Then lead kids to say the verse together, using hand motions to remember specific words. Begin with these four motions:

1. *teaching*: hold palms together and open like a book
2. *fellowship*: wave to others in the room
3. *breaking of bread*: play out tearing apart bread
4. *prayers*: fold hands together as if praying

Explain that *fellowship* means spending time together as

friends, and *breaking of bread* means eating meals together, including the Lord's Supper.

Invite kids to sing together the song "Every Day."

Leader •Great job. Let's work hard to memorize our key passage. By memorizing verses from the Bible, we fill our minds with God's Word. Learning Scripture will help us think and act like Jesus, and remember the truth about God, ourselves, and the world around us.

Discussion starter video (5 minutes)

• "Unit 34 Session 1" discussion starter video

Leader •The Book of Acts tells us what the early church was like. Check out this video.

Show the "Unit 34 Session 1" video.

Leader •The early church shared what they had and took care of each others' needs. What can you share to help people in need?

Sing (3 minutes)

• "Build Your Kingdom Here" song

Leader •When people trust in Jesus as Lord and Savior, God changes them. Believers didn't share because they *had* to; they shared because they *wanted* to! God's power in the Holy Spirit works through believers still today. The Holy Spirit gives us power to tell others about Jesus and show them His love. Let's sing!

Lead boys and girls to sing together "Build Your Kingdom Here."

Prayer (2 minutes)

Before dismissing to small groups, pray and thank God for blessing the believers in the early church. Praise Him for working in believers today through the Holy Spirit.

Dismiss to small groups

The Gospel: God's Plan for Me

Ask kids if they have ever heard the word *gospel*. Clarify that the word *gospel* means "good news." It is the message about Christ, the kingdom of God, and salvation. Use the following guide to share the gospel with kids.

God rules. Explain to kids that the Bible tells us God created everything, and He is in charge of everything. Invite a volunteer to read Genesis 1:1 from the Bible. Read Revelation 4:11 or Colossians 1:16-17 aloud and explain what these verses mean.

We sinned. Tell kids that since the time of Adam and Eve, everyone has chosen to disobey God. (Romans 3:23) The Bible calls this sin. Because God is holy, God cannot be around sin. Sin separates us from God and deserves God's punishment of death. (Romans 6:23)

God provided. Choose a child to read John 3:16 aloud. Say that God sent His Son, Jesus, the perfect solution to our sin problem, to rescue us from the punishment we deserve. It's something we, as sinners, could never earn on our own. Jesus alone saves us. Read and explain Ephesians 2:8-9.

Jesus gives. Share with kids that Jesus lived a perfect life, died on the cross for our sins, and rose again. Because Jesus gave up His life for us, we can be welcomed into God's family for eternity. This is the best gift ever! Read Romans 5:8; 2 Corinthians 5:21; or 1 Peter 3:18.

We respond. Tell kids that they can respond to Jesus. Read Romans 10:9-10,13. Review these aspects of our response: Believe in your heart that Jesus alone saves you through what He's already done on the cross. Repent, turning from self and sin to Jesus. Tell God and others that your faith is in Jesus.

Offer to talk with any child who is interested in responding to Jesus.

Small Group LEADER

Session Title: The Church Met Needs
Bible Passage: Acts 3:1-10; 4:32-37
Big Picture Question: By whose power did Peter heal the man who was lame? Peter healed the man by the power of Jesus.
Key Passage: Acts 2:42,47
Unit Christ Connection: The church is God's plan to bring praise and glory to Jesus.

Key passage activity (5 minutes)

• Key Passage Poster

Lead kids to say the verse together, using the hand motions created during large group. Explain that you will describe someone from the Bible story, and kids should read the key passage as if they are that person.

- • the beggar who couldn't walk (*quietly, sad*)
- • the healed man (*loudly, happy*)
- • the amazed crowd (*with awe and surprise*)

Say • Very good! These verses tell us about the early church. God blessed them, and the church grew. Let's all try to memorize our key passage this week.

Bible story review & Bible skills (10 minutes)

• Bibles, 1 per kid
• Small Group Visual Pack
• index cards
• large sheet of paper
• marker

Option: Retell or review the Bible story using the bolded text of the Bible story script.

Write various point values on separate index cards. Include both positive and negative values. Stack the cards facedown.

Form two teams. Invite the first team to answer a review question. If the team is correct, they may draw a point card. Keep track of teams' totals on a large sheet of paper. The team that answered correctly may choose to play again, or pass play to the next team. Warn the teams that some point values are negative, so playing again may or may not give them an advantage of earning more points!

Sample questions:

1. Which of Jesus' followers went to the temple? (*Peter and John, Acts 3:1*)
2. What was wrong with the man at the gate? (*He was lame, he could not walk; Acts 3:2*)
3. What was the name of the gate? (*the Beautiful Gate, Acts 3:2*)
4. What did the man want from the passersby? (*money or alms, Acts 3:2*)
5. What did Peter give the man? (*healing, Acts 3:6*)
6. ***By whose power did Peter heal the man who was lame? Peter healed the man by the power of Jesus.***
7. What did the man do in the temple? (*walked, leapt, and praised God; Acts 3:8*)
8. What did the early believers do with their possessions? (*shared them, Acts 4:32*)

If you choose to review with boys and girls how to become a Christian, explain that kids are welcome to speak with you or another teacher if they have questions.

- **God rules.** God created and is in charge of everything. (Gen. 1:1; Rev. 4:11; Col. 1:16-17)
- **We sinned.** Since Adam and Eve, everyone has chosen to disobey God. (Rom. 3:23; 6:23)
- **God provided.** God sent His Son, Jesus, to rescue us from the punishment we deserve. (John 3:16; Eph. 2:8-9)
- **Jesus gives.** Jesus lived a perfect life, died on the cross for our sins, and rose again so we can be welcomed into God's family. (Rom. 5:8; 2 Cor. 5:21; 1 Pet. 3:18)
- **We respond.** Believe that Jesus alone saves you. Repent. Tell God that your faith is in Jesus. (Rom. 10:9-10,13)

• sticky notes
• markers

Tip: Do not use items that could be easily lost or broken.

Activity choice (10 minutes)

Option 1: What's mine is yours

Guide each kid to use a sticky note to label a personal item (shoe, favorite pencil, Bible, and so forth) with his name. If kids do not have an item, offer a classroom object.

Collect the items and display them at the front of the room. Point out how lovely or interesting some of the items are. Invite kids to tell where they got the items or why the items are their favorites. Then distribute the items to kids so each item goes to someone whose name is not on the item.

Say • How does it feel to see someone else with something that belonged to you? [*Allow kids to respond.*] Raise your hand if you want your stuff back.

• The Bible says that the believers in the early church lived as if they were all one big family; they shared everything. No one ever said, "That's mine! You can't have it!" (Acts 4:32).

Be sure to return the items to their original owners.

Option 2: What I have, I give you

• playing cards

Invite kids to play a game similar to "Go Fish." Give each player five cards. Explain that kids should lay down any pairs of numbers that match. Then give them more cards until everyone has five cards that do not match.

To begin, the first player will look at any other player and ask for a card he needs: "Do you have any 4s?"

If the other player has a 4, she should give that card to the first player. He will lay down his match, and play moves left to the next player. If the other player does not have the card she is asked for, instead of saying, "Go fish," she should say, "I do not have a 4, but what I have, I give you." Then she should give him one of her cards.

Whenever a player gives away a card or lays down a

pair, he should pick up more cards from the pile so he always has five cards in his hand. Continue play as time allows or until kids run out of cards.

Say • Do you remember what the man at the temple gate wanted? (*money*) Peter said, "I don't have silver or gold, but what I have, I give you."

• What did Peter give the man? (*healing*)

• ***By whose power did Peter heal the man who was lame? Peter healed the man by the power of Jesus.***

Journal and prayer (5 minutes)

• pencils
• journals
• Bibles
• Journal Page, 1 per kid (enhanced CD)
• "Meeting Needs" activity page, 1 per kid

Tip: Each quarter, the *Older Kids Activity Pack* includes a set of *Big Picture Cards for Families.* Give the card pack to parents today to allow families to interact with the biblical content each week.

Distribute pencils and journal pages. Prompt kids to draw a picture of a possession they value a lot. Ask them to think about whether or not they would share that possession. How should believers respond to people in need?

Say • The early church met needs. By healing the man who was lame, Peter showed how powerful Jesus is. ***By whose power did Peter heal the man who was lame? Peter healed the man by the power of Jesus.***

• The believers in the early church shared what they had. Jesus gives believers the greatest gift—salvation from sin! Jesus didn't say, "That's mine! You can't have it!" when God sent Him to earth to give up His life for us. Jesus gave up everything to rescue us from sin and death.

Invite kids to share prayer requests. Close the group in prayer, or allow a couple volunteers to pray.

As time allows, lead kids to complete the activity page "Meeting Needs." Kids will follow each path, picking up letters along the way to fill in the message. (*God gives the Holy Spirit to believers today so the church can tell others about Jesus and show them His love.*)

Leader BIBLE STUDY

There were two groups of Jews in the first church: Hellenistic Jews (Jews who spoke Greek) and Hebraic Jews (Jews who spoke Hebrew). The Greek-speaking Jews were from foreign countries, and the Hebrew-speaking Jews had been born in Israel. In those early days, as the apostles faithfully taught and preached the gospel, the church grew quickly.

2 But tension existed between the two groups. Perhaps the Hebraic Jews considered themselves superior to the Hellenistic Jews, or maybe the groups lacked communication. In any case, the Hellenistic Jews complained that their widows were not being cared for properly.

The Old Testament law was clear about what God requires of His people. He commanded them to care for the orphans and widows. (See Ex. 22:22; Deut. 10:18.) The early church continued this Jewish custom, but there was a problem. The Greek-speaking Jews claimed their widows were not getting their share of the daily distributions.

The twelve apostles were quick to address the issue. They gathered all the believers together. The apostles explained that God had called them to preaching and teaching. They were not above handling problems among the people, but they wisely led the church to choose seven leaders to oversee such duties.

The church did not choose just anyone to serve; the men were reputable, full of the Spirit, and wise. The chosen seven were Stephen, Philip, Prochorus (PRAHK uh ruhs), Nicanor (nigh KAY nawr), Timon (TIGH mahn), Parmenas (PAHR mih nuhs), and Nicolaus (NIK uh LAY uhs). Now the apostles were free to devote themselves to prayer and preaching, and the widows were properly cared for.

Everyone in the church has a role in God's work. The seven men who were chosen used their abilities to take care of others, and the apostles kept teaching the Word of God. Many people heard the Word of God and came to believe and trust in Jesus.

Older Kids BIBLE STUDY OVERVIEW

Session Title: Seven Men Were Chosen
Bible Passage: Acts 6:1-7
Big Picture Question: Who can do God's work? God gives every believer skills for doing His work.
Key Passage: Acts 2:42,47
Unit Christ Connection: The church is God's plan to bring praise and glory to Jesus.

Small Group Opening

Large Group Leader

Small Group Leader

Additional suggestions for specific groups are available at *gospelproject.com/kids/additional-resources*.

For free online training on how to lead a group, visit *ministrygrid.com/web/thegospelproject*.

The BIBLE STORY

Seven Men Were Chosen
Acts 6:1-7

In the time **after Jesus' resurrection and return to heaven, more and more people believed in Him. But some of the believers complained.** The Jews who spoke Greek complained about the Jews who spoke Hebrew. **The Greek-speaking Jews thought the widows were being overlooked when the daily food was given out.** In the Old Testament, God told His people to take care of widows—women whose husbands had died.

The twelve apostles gathered all the believers together. (Matthias had been chosen to replace Judas.) **They said, "It isn't right for us to stop preaching about God to take care of all these daily things. So, brothers, choose seven men to take care of this."**

The apostles said that the men should be good men—men who are wise and full of the Holy Spirit. These men should be obedient to God and be able to make good choices. **These seven men would take care of the daily business of the believers. Then the apostles could devote themselves to prayer and to preaching.** Both jobs were important, but the apostles should not stop teaching God's Word because hearing the Word was how people believed.

Everyone agreed that this was a good idea. So they chose seven men: Stephen, Philip, Prochorus (PRAHK uh ruhs), **Nicanor** (nigh KAY nawr), **Timon** (TIGH mahn), **Parmenas** (PAHR mih nuhs), **and Nicolaus** (NIK uh LAY uhs). These men stood before Jesus' disciples, who prayed for them and laid their hands on them.

So the twelve apostles kept preaching about God. More and more people heard the truth about God, and more and more people in Jerusalem believed in Him.

Christ Connection: The apostles believed that everyone in the church had an important job to do to serve God's people and help spread the gospel. Jesus wants us to serve others so that the message of His death and resurrection can be heard and believed all over the world.

Want to discover God's Word? Get *Bible Express*!
Invite kids to check out today's devotional to discover how we obey God out of love for Him. (See 1 John 2:5.) The seven men who were chosen to serve the church did so out of love for God and His people. We don't serve God to earn His love; His love is freely given! For more information, check out *www.lifeway.com/devotionals*.

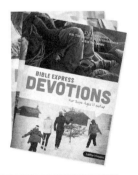

Small Group OPENING

Session Title: Seven Men Were Chosen
Bible Passage: Acts 6:1-7
Big Picture Question: Who can do God's work? God gives every believer skills for doing His work.
Key Passage: Acts 2:42,47
Unit Christ Connection: The church is God's plan to bring praise and glory to Jesus.

Welcome time

Greet each kid as he or she arrives. Use this time to collect the offering, fill out attendance sheets, and help new kids connect to your group. Prompt kids to share about a time they have worked with or played on a team. What task or activity did the team accomplish?

Activity page (5 minutes)

- "I Choose You!" activity page, 1 per kid
- pencils

Distribute the activity page and guide kids to use the code to fill in the spaces. The first number in the code tells you which name to look at in the roll call list, and the second number tells you which letter of that name to use.

For example, 1-3 tells you to go to the first name, *Stephen*, and use the third letter, *E*.

Say • Did anyone figure out what today's Bible story is about? (*Seven men were chosen to be leaders in the church.*)

Session starter (10 minutes)

Option 1: List seven

- pencils
- paper

Give each kid a piece of paper and a pencil. Explain that you will name a category, and kids should list seven items that fit in that category. When kids finish, call on someone to name something on his list. Any other kids who wrote down that same item should cross it off their lists. Continue naming items, applauding kids for creativity and originality.

Play again with new categories as time allows:

- Pizza toppings
- Kinds of candy
- Things in the sky
- Things you wear
- Musical instruments

Say • You are all so creative! Today's Bible story includes a list of some more things—names of men who were chosen to help at church. Do you know how many men were chosen? That's right—seven!

Option 2: Seven questions

- classroom objects or common household objects, 7
- index cards
- marker

Display at the front of the room seven various classroom or common household objects. (Examples: books, tissue boxes, telephones, clothes hangers, pens, ball caps, calculators, erasers, hairbrushes, staplers, or so on)

Write the name of an object on an index card and turn it facedown. Tell kids that you have one of these objects in mind. Challenge kids to ask seven yes-or-no questions to figure out what object you have chosen. Call on kids one at a time to ask a question. When a kid guesses the object, choose another and play again as time allows.

Say • Very good questions and great guessing! Keep the number seven in mind as we get ready to hear the Bible story today. In the story, seven people were chosen for a special purpose.

Transition to large group

The Early Church

Large Group LEADER

Session Title: Seven Men Were Chosen
Bible Passage: Acts 6:1-7
Big Picture Question: Who can do God's work? God gives every believer skills for doing His work.
Key Passage: Acts 2:42,47
Unit Christ Connection: The church is God's plan to bring praise and glory to Jesus.

Countdown

• countdown video

Show the countdown video as your kids arrive, and set it to end as large group time begins.

Introduce the session (3 minutes)

• leader attire
• safety glasses
• hard hat
• clipboard

[Large Group Leader enters wearing safety glasses and a hard hat. He or she is carrying a clipboard and flipping through a couple of papers on it.]

Leader •Oh! Hello, everyone! Welcome back. I sure am glad you are here. I have to tell you that I really appreciated your help last time choosing a plan for the tree house I am building. I selected a plan that I think is going to be just perfect! It has everything you could ever want in a tree house—a balcony, a rope bridge, windows, bunk beds, a staircase, and a secret hatch!

Anyway, construction is underway! The only problem is that I can't possibly build all of these parts myself! What I could really use is some professional help. [*Look at clipboard.*] Say, can any of you recommend a good plumber? Or a skilled electrician? Raise your hand if you have experience with a laser-precise compound miter saw.

Timeline map (1 minute)

• Timeline Map

Leader • Looks like I'm going to spend the day searching for some special helpers to build my tree house. In the meantime, let's get ready for today's Bible story! Last time, we heard a story about the early church and how the believers helped people. Today we are going to hear about some of the work the believers in the early church did. Here is our story: "Seven Men Were Chosen."

Big picture question (1 minute)

Leader • Wow! Seven men … they must have had a big job to do. I think I could get this tree house built with about five helpers. I mean, they'd have to be *expert* helpers. You can't hire just anyone to do the work of building a tree house. You know, you wouldn't want to hire a baby. No offense to babies, but you can't hand a baby a screwdriver and expect anything to get done.

I wonder if the leaders of the early church had that problem. They had work to do, but who could help? As we listen to the Bible story, see if you can figure out the answer to our big picture question. Here it is: ***Who can do God's work?***

Tell the Bible story (10 minutes)

• "Seven Men Were Chosen" video
• Bibles, 1 per kid
• Bible Story Picture Slide or Poster
• Big Picture Question Slide or Poster

Open your Bible to Acts 6:1-7 and tell the Bible story in your own words, or show the Bible story video "Seven Men Were Chosen."

Leader • In the early days of the church, many people believed in Jesus and the church grew. The believers in the church helped each other and shared what they had if someone had a need. But it sounds like there was a problem! Some of the believers said that the widows were not being cared for properly. Maybe they didn't get

Note: The term *apostle* refers to someone who is sent on a mission, like the Twelve whom Jesus called and sent. *Disciple* refers to any believer who helps spread the good news about Jesus.

enough food when it was distributed every day.

So the leaders in the church—the twelve apostles—gathered together all the believers. They needed to choose some helpers because if they stopped preaching to make sure everyone got what he or she needed, then who would be preaching? It's not that they were too important to handle these types of problems; they needed to keep doing what God had called them to do. God had given them skills so they were good at preaching.

So they told the believers to choose seven men to help in the church. These were men who had special skills to do God's work. They helped serve the other believers. That leads me to our big picture question, ***Who can do God's work?*** Do you know the answer? ***God gives every believer skills for doing His work.*** Let's say that together. ***Who can do God's work? God gives every believer skills for doing His work.***

What kind of special skills did these seven men have? The Bible says that they had good reputations, were filled with the Holy Spirit, and were wise.

Everyone in the church has a role in God's work. The seven men who were chosen used their abilities to take care of others, and the apostles kept teaching the Word of God. Many people heard the Word of God and came to believe and trust in Jesus. ***Who can do God's work? God gives every believer skills for doing His work.***

The Gospel: God's Plan for Me (optional)

Using Scripture and the guide provided, explain to boys and girls how to become a Christian. Tell kids how they can respond, and provide counselors to speak with each kid individually. Guide counselors to use open-ended questions to allow kids to determine the direction of the conversation.

Encourage boys and girls to ask their parents, small group leaders, or other adults any questions they may have about becoming a Christian.

Key passage (5 minutes)

• Key Passage Slide or Poster
• "Every Day" song
• Bible

Leader • Does anyone remember our key passage? It tells us about some of the things the believers in the early church did.

Invite any kids who have memorized the key passage to recite it aloud. Then display the key passage poster. Show the kids where to find Acts 2 in the Bible.

Lead the kids in reading the key passage aloud. You may choose to use any hand motions created in the previous week with the key words.

Leader • Did you notice how the church grew? As the believers were obedient to tell others about Jesus, God added to their number. People heard the gospel—the good news about Jesus—and they believed. God saved them from their sins! Let's sing.

Guide boys and girls to sing together "Every Day."

Discussion starter video (5 minutes)

• "Unit 34 Session 2" discussion starter video

Leader • Since God gives every believers skills for doing His work, everyone can help at church! Let's watch.

Show the "Unit 34 Session 2" video.

Leader • Who would you choose to help at church? Can you think of specific people who you see helping at our church? What jobs do they do?

Lead kids to discuss ways they might help at your church. Allow them to share experiences they've had helping at church or skills they have that might be useful for serving others. What skills do they see in each other?

Sing (3 minutes)

• "Build Your
Kingdom Here" song

Leader • God builds His kingdom through the church. God uses the believers in the church to accomplish His work. *Who can do God's work? God gives every believer skills for doing His work.*

Allow a volunteer to help lead the group in singing the unit theme song "Build Your Kingdom Here."

Prayer (2 minutes)

Leader • Thanks, everyone, for your attention today. Come back next time and maybe I will have my tree house finished! Before you go, let's pray.

Lead the group in prayer, asking God to give kids opportunities at church to serve Him and others. Pray that kids would serve selflessly, desiring to bring glory to Him rather than themselves. Acknowledge that God does not need us to accomplish His will, but thank Him for using us to do His work.

Dismiss to small groups

The Gospel: God's Plan for Me

Ask kids if they have ever heard the word *gospel*. Clarify that the word *gospel* means "good news." It is the message about Christ, the kingdom of God, and salvation. Use the following guide to share the gospel with kids.

God rules. Explain to kids that the Bible tells us God created everything, and He is in charge of everything. Invite a volunteer to read Genesis 1:1 from the Bible. Read Revelation 4:11 or Colossians 1:16-17 aloud and explain what these verses mean.

We sinned. Tell kids that since the time of Adam and Eve, everyone has chosen to disobey God. (Romans 3:23) The Bible calls this sin. Because God is holy, God cannot be around sin. Sin separates us from God and deserves God's punishment of death. (Romans 6:23)

God provided. Choose a child to read John 3:16 aloud. Say that God sent His Son, Jesus, the perfect solution to our sin problem, to rescue us from the punishment we deserve. It's something we, as sinners, could never earn on our own. Jesus alone saves us. Read and explain Ephesians 2:8-9.

Jesus gives. Share with kids that Jesus lived a perfect life, died on the cross for our sins, and rose again. Because Jesus gave up His life for us, we can be welcomed into God's family for eternity. This is the best gift ever! Read Romans 5:8; 2 Corinthians 5:21; or 1 Peter 3:18.

We respond. Tell kids that they can respond to Jesus. Read Romans 10:9-10,13. Review these aspects of our response: Believe in your heart that Jesus alone saves you through what He's already done on the cross. Repent, turning from self and sin to Jesus. Tell God and others that your faith is in Jesus.

Offer to talk with any child who is interested in responding to Jesus.

Small Group LEADER

Session Title: Seven Men Were Chosen
Bible Passage: Acts 6:1-7
Big Picture Question: Who can do God's work? God gives every believer skills for doing His work.
Key Passage: Acts 2:42,47
Unit Christ Connection: The church is God's plan to bring praise and glory to Jesus.

Key passage activity (5 minutes)

• Key Passage Poster
• dry erase board
• dry erase markers

Display the key passage poster and lead the group to read it aloud together. Then write the first two letters of each word on a dry erase board. Hide the poster and challenge kids to say the verse from memory, using the letters as hints. As kids master the verse, erase sets of letters.

Say • Nice work. Keep trying to memorize our key passage. We'll say it again next week. It tells us some of the things the believers in the early church did. They faithfully served God, and God blessed them. More people were saved every day.

Bible story review & Bible skills (10 minutes)

• Bibles, 1 per kid
• Small Group Visual Pack
• beach ball
• permanent marker

Option: Retell or review the Bible story using the bolded text of the Bible story script.

Use a permanent marker to write the numbers *1* through *7* in a scattered formation on a beach ball.

Invite kids to stand in a circle. Give the ball to one player to begin. He will toss the ball to another player in the group. That player should catch the ball and then look to see which number is closest to her left thumb. Based on the number, ask a review question or give one of the following prompts to review the Bible story. Then she will pass the ball to another player, and play continues.

1. Name one of the seven men chosen to help. (*Stephen, Philip, Prochorus, Nicanor, Timon, Parmenas, Nicolaus; Acts 6:5*)
2. Name one of the groups of people in the story. (*Jews who spoke Greek, Jews who spoke Hebrew, widows, twelve apostles, all the believers, the seven men*)
3. Name one trait of a good church leader. (*filled with the Holy Spirit, has a good reputation, is wise; Acts 6:3*)
4. ***Who can do God's work? God gives every believer skills for doing His work.***
5. Retell the story in your own words.
6. What tasks did the apostles need to focus on? (*prayer and preaching, Acts 6:4*)
7. What happened after the seven started helping the church? (*The apostles kept preaching. More people heard the truth about God and believed in Him; Acts 6:7*)

Say
- Everyone in the church has an important job to do. God makes some people good at preaching, and others are good at other things like teaching or serving or handling money.
- We can all work together to serve God's people and help spread the gospel. Jesus wants us to serve others so that the message of His death and resurrection can be heard and believed all over the world.

If you choose to review with boys and girls how to become a Christian, explain that kids are welcome to speak with you or another teacher if they have questions.

- **God rules.** God created and is in charge of everything. (Gen. 1:1; Rev. 4:11; Col. 1:16-17)
- **We sinned.** Since Adam and Eve, everyone has chosen to disobey God. (Rom. 3:23; 6:23)

- **God provided.** God sent His Son, Jesus, to rescue us from the punishment we deserve. (John 3:16; Eph. 2:8-9)
- **Jesus gives.** Jesus lived a perfect life, died on the cross for our sins, and rose again so we can be welcomed into God's family. (Rom. 5:8; 2 Cor. 5:21; 1 Pet. 3:18)
- **We respond.** Believe that Jesus alone saves you. Repent. Tell God that your faith is in Jesus. (Rom. 10:9-10,13)

Activity choice (10 minutes)

• index cards
• markers

Option 1: Helpers charades

Write on separate index cards some jobs people can do to help at church. Stack them facedown. Invite kids one at a time to pick a card and silently act out the job. The rest of the kids should try to guess what job is on the card.

Suggestions: *take up the offering*, *pass out bulletins*, *open doors*, *sing*, *pray*, *teach a class*, *care for babies*, *greet visitors*, *sweep floors*, *serve food*, and so forth.

Say •*Who can do God's work? God gives every believer skills for doing His work.*

Option 2: Service relay

• chairs
• paper plates, 1 per team
• table tennis balls, 7 per team
• painter's tape

Use tape to mark a start line on the floor at one end of the room. At the other end of the room, position two chairs. At each chair, position seven table tennis balls.

Form teams of seven kids each. Guide each team to stand single file behind the start line. Give the first player in each line a paper plate. When you say go, the first players should walk quickly to the chair, put one ball on the plate, and return to their teams. Each player will pass the plate to the next player, who will go to pick up a second ball.

Players will continue relaying until the last player brings all seven balls back to the team. If a ball falls, the player should stop and pick it up. When every player has raced, the team should sit down.

Say • Great job working together! Believers in a church can work together to serve God's people and help spread the gospel. ***Who can do God's work? God gives every believer skills for doing His work.***

• Jesus wants us to serve others so that the message of His death and resurrection can be heard and believed all over the world.

Journal and prayer (5 minutes)

• pencils
• journals
• Bibles
• Journal Page, 1 per kid (enhanced CD)
• "Wanted: Church Leader" activity page, 1 per kid

Distribute journals and pencils to boys and girls. Encourage each kid to write or draw a picture of something he could do to help at church. (Examples: opening doors for guests, passing out bulletins, sending cards to visitors or members, and so forth)

Consider compiling a list of specific needs at your church that kids could help meet.

Say • ***Who can do God's work? God gives every believer skills for doing His work.***

Invite kids to share any prayer requests they have. Close in prayer, mentioning the prayer requests and thanking God for the church. Thank Him for giving every believer special gifts and abilities to serve in the church so people can hear the good news about Jesus, believe, and be saved.

As time allows, lead kids to complete the activity page "Wanted: Church Leader." The hidden words describe qualities of a good church leader, based on 1 Timothy 3:1-7.

Leader BIBLE STUDY

Stephen was one of the seven men chosen to serve as leaders in the early church at Jerusalem. (See Acts 6:1-7.) God blessed Stephen, and God gave him power to do wonders and miracles like some of the apostles.

Some of the Jews argued with Stephen. They accused him of blasphemy and dragged him to the Sanhedrin, a group of Jewish leaders that acted as a legal council. As accusations were presented to the council, everyone at the meeting looked at Stephen, and his face looked like the face of an angel.

3 Stephen addressed the group. He drew from the Jewish history which the leaders in the Sanhedrin would have known well. But Stephen taught from the Old Testament things the Jewish leaders had likely never realized. He reminded them of Abraham's faith in God and of Joseph's plight in Egypt. He talked about Moses and the Israelites who rejected God's plan. But God did not give up on them.

As Stephen preached, he showed how the Old Testament pointed to a coming Savior and how that Savior was Jesus. Stephen pointed out that the Jews' ancestors had rejected God's prophets. And they were just like their fathers; they rejected the Messiah, the Lord Jesus. Not only did they reject Jesus, they killed Him!

The Jewish leaders were angry! They rushed at Stephen. The Holy Spirit filled Stephen, and he looked into heaven. He saw God's glory, and Jesus was standing at God's right hand. The Jews forced Stephen out of the city, and they stoned him. As he died, Stephen called out, "Lord, do not charge them with this sin!"

Stephen was killed because he was a Christian. Jesus told His followers that they would be persecuted—hated, hurt, or even killed—for loving Him. (Mark 13:9-13; John 16:2) Jesus also said that those who suffer for Him would be blessed. (Matthew 5:11) Stephen was not afraid to die because he saw Jesus waiting for him in heaven. We can face suffering in this life because we know great joy is waiting for us in heaven.

Older Kids BIBLE STUDY OVERVIEW

Session Title: Stephen's Address
Bible Passage: Acts 6:8–7:60
Big Picture Question: Why was Stephen not afraid to die? Stephen saw
   Jesus waiting for him in heaven.
Key Passage: Acts 2:42,47
Unit Christ Connection: The church is God's plan to bring praise and
   glory to Jesus.

3

Small Group Opening

Large Group Leader

Small Group Leader

Additional suggestions for specific groups are available at *gospelproject.com/kids/additional-resources*.

For free online training on how to lead a group, visit *ministrygrid.com/web/thegospelproject*.

The BIBLE STORY

Stephen's Address
Acts 6:8–7:60

One of Jesus' followers was named Stephen. God blessed Stephen and gave him power to do great wonders and signs among the people in Jerusalem. **One day, some Jews came and began to argue with Stephen.** No matter how hard the Jews tried, they could not win the argument. The Holy Spirit helped Stephen, and he spoke with wisdom.

So **the Jews got a group of men together, and they lied about Stephen.** They said that Stephen had spoken against God. **The people dragged Stephen to** the Sanhedrin (san HEE drihn), which was **the Jewish court.** There, they told more lies about Stephen. **"We heard him say that Jesus will destroy this place and change the laws that Moses gave us," they said.**

"Is this true?" the high priest asked Stephen.

Stephen began to preach to them about Jesus. He started by reminding them about Abraham. God had made promises to Abraham and to his son Isaac. He reminded them about Joseph and Moses. God kept Joseph safe when his brothers tried to hurt him, and God used Joseph to help all His people during a famine. God's people lived in Egypt. A new ruler made God's people slaves and treated them badly. God called Moses to rescue His people from Pharaoh. Moses led God's people away from Egypt, but they turned against Moses and they turned against God.

God did not give up on His people, though. He was working out a plan. God worked through Joshua and David and Solomon. The religious leaders knew these stories from the Old Testament.

Stephen told them these **stories to explain that the Messiah God had promised was Jesus! But just like their ancestors rejected and killed the prophets in the Old Testament, these Jewish leaders had rejected Jesus and murdered Him!**

When the Jewish leaders heard the things Stephen accused them of, they were so angry! Stephen was filled with the Holy Spirit, and he **looked up into heaven. Stephen saw Jesus standing there.**

"Look!" he said. "I see the heavens opened and the Son of Man standing at the right hand of God!"

The Jewish leaders screamed at the top of their lungs. They covered their ears and **rushed at Stephen. They threw Stephen out of the city and began to throw stones at him.** The people who saw this happen laid their robes at the feet of a young man named Saul. As they were stoning him, **Stephen called out, "Lord Jesus, receive my spirit!" Then Stephen knelt down and cried out with a loud voice, "Lord, do not hold this sin against them!" After saying this, Stephen died.**

Christ Connection: Stephen was killed because he was a Christian. Jesus told His followers that they would be persecuted—hated, hurt, or even killed—for loving Him. Jesus also said that those who suffer for Him would be blessed. (Matthew 5:11) We can face suffering in this life because Jesus suffered first. He died and then rose again, and He is waiting for us in heaven.

Want to discover God's Word? Get *Bible Express*!
Invite kids to check out today's devotional to discover how God views the church: as one body. (Romans 12:5) Stephen's death was a sad experience in the early church, but God used his death to bring more people into His church. As a church, we can love and care for each other. Order in bulk, subscribe quarterly, or purchase individually. For more information, check out *www.lifeway.com/devotionals*.

Small Group OPENING

Session Title: Stephen's Address
Bible Passage: Acts 6:8–7:60
Big Picture Question: Why was Stephen not afraid to die? Stephen saw Jesus waiting for him in heaven.
Key Passage: Acts 2:42,47
Unit Christ Connection: The church is God's plan to bring praise and glory to Jesus.

Welcome time

Greet each kid as he or she arrives. Use this time to collect the offering, fill out attendance sheets, and help new kids connect to your group. Invite kids to tell about a time they felt afraid. What did they do?

Activity page (5 minutes)

- "History Match" activity page, 1 per kid
- pencils

Challenge kids to review some Old Testament stories on the activity page. Kids should match each person in the Old Testament with a description given in the Book of Acts.

If kids need help, guide them to find and read the verses in their Bibles. (*King Solomon, Acts 7:47; King David, Acts 7:46; Joseph, Acts 7:9-10; Moses, Acts 7:30-32*)

Say • The Bible story we will hear today comes from the New Testament, but someone talked a lot about the events of the Old Testament, including these!

Session starter (10 minutes)

Option 1: I'm not afraid!

Instruct boys and girls to sit in a circle. Choose one kid to play first. Ask him to complete the statement, "I'm not afraid of … " (Example: "I'm not afraid of the dark.")

Explain that any kids who agree with the statement should stand up. Lead all the kids standing to say, "Don't be afraid! God is in control." Then guide everyone to sit. Give the next kid a turn to complete the statement. Continue around the circle as time allows.

Say • Some things in life do make us feel afraid because we aren't sure what is going to happen. But today we are going to hear a Bible story about something no one needs to fear if they trust in Jesus.

Option 2: Take a stand

• hula hoops, 2
• gift bag
• index cards
• marker

Prepare by writing simple group actions on several index cards. (Suggestions: *Do 5 jumping jacks*, *give a friend a high-five*, *jump as high as you can*, *say the alphabet as quickly as you can*, and so forth.) Put the action cards in a bag. Position two hula hoops on the floor, several feet apart.

Guide kids to stand. Explain that you read a statement. If kids agree, they should put one foot in the first hula hoop. If they disagree, they should put one foot in the second hula hoop. After kids have moved to a hoop, pull a card from the bag and instruct all the kids at the first hoop to do the action. Then play again with another statement and another card. Each time, the first group should complete the action.

Sample statements:
• I think that dogs are the best animals in the world.
• My favorite food is pizza.
• Math is my favorite subject in school.

Say • Did any of you disagree with the statement just so you could avoid doing the action? In today's Bible story, a man took a stand for what he believed even though it cost him everything.

Transition to large group

Large Group LEADER

Session Title: Stephen's Address
Bible Passage: Acts 6:8–7:60
Big Picture Question: Why was Stephen not afraid to die? Stephen saw Jesus waiting for him in heaven.
Key Passage: Acts 2:42,47
Unit Christ Connection: The church is God's plan to bring praise and glory to Jesus.

Countdown

• countdown video

Show the countdown video as your kids arrive, and set it to end as large group time begins.

Introduce the session (3 minutes)

• leader attire

[Large Group Leader enters waving his or her arms and skipping around with much excitement.]

Leader • It's finished! It's finished! We did it! We did it! Oh, boy! I am so excited. The tree house I have been planning and building and working on is finally finished! I put the last coat of paint on the outside earlier today, and let me tell you … it is *beautiful*! This is definitely the best-looking tree house I have ever seen in my entire life.

Whew! Maybe if we have time later, I can show it to you. You can climb up the rope ladder and look out over the balcony … hey, you aren't afraid of heights are you? Raise your hand if you're not afraid of heights. Well, even if you are, that's OK. I can just show you a picture of the tree house instead.

For now, let me tell you a Bible story. It's about a guy who was in a scary situation. Do you think he was scared?

Timeline map (1 minute)

• Timeline Map

Leader •Let's see here. Last time we heard a story about the early church and how seven men were chosen to help serve in the church. One of the men chosen was named Stephen, and he is in our Bible story today. It's called "Stephen's Address." I don't mean mailing address, like where Stephen lived. *Address* is another word for *speech*. Do you see anyone who looks like he is giving a speech?

Here it is! This must be Stephen because he is speaking to a crowd, but that crowd sure looks angry!

Big picture question (1 minute)

Leader •OK, this does look like a scary situation for Stephen! While you listen to the Bible story, listen for the answer to our big picture question: *Why was Stephen not afraid to die?* Oh, man! Stephen was going to die? Things are not looking good for Stephen. Let's get started.

Tell the Bible story (10 minutes)

• "Stephen's Address" video
• Bibles, 1 per kid
• Bible Story Picture Slide or Poster
• Big Picture Question Slide or Poster

Open your Bible to Acts 6:8–7:60 and tell the Bible story in your own words, or show the Bible story video "Stephen's Address."

Leader •Stephen was a believer. He followed Jesus' teachings and told others about Him. Stephen had good news to share, but some of the Jews did not like this news. They didn't believe Jesus is God's Son. They accused him of blasphemy, or saying something about God that is not true, and they dragged him to the Jewish court.

Stephen preached to the Jewish leaders. They knew the Old Testament; it was part of their Jewish history. But Stephen said that the Old Testament pointed to a coming Savior, and he said that Savior is Jesus. He told the leaders that they were just like their ancestors who hurt and killed God's prophets who told about Jesus. But what these Jewish leaders had done was worse. When the One whom God had promised came to earth, they rejected Jesus and killed Him! Now the Jewish leaders were really mad. They wanted to kill Stephen, so they forced him out of the city and began to throw stones at him.

The Bible says that the Holy Spirit filled Stephen, and when Stephen looked into heaven, he saw Jesus standing at God's right hand. As he died, Stephen asked God not to hold the sin of his accusers against them.

Stephen was brave before his enemies. He did not take back what he said about Jesus. He did not change his mind about what he believed. If he had, maybe they would have stopped hurting him. Maybe if Stephen had said, "Never mind, I agree with you that Jesus is not the Son of God," maybe he would have lived. But that is not the truth. Jesus *is* the Son of God, and Stephen was brave to die for the name of Jesus. He was not afraid to die.

Why was Stephen not afraid to die? Stephen saw Jesus waiting for him in heaven.

Stephen faced persecution. *Persecution* is when someone is hated, hurt, or killed for what he or she believes. Jesus said that people who believe in Him will be persecuted in this life. They will suffer because they trust in Jesus. But we can face suffering because, like Stephen, we know that there is great joy waiting for us in heaven. Those who trust in Jesus will live with Him forever.

The Gospel: God's Plan for Me (optional)

Using Scripture and the guide provided, explain to boys and girls how to become a Christian. Tell kids how they can respond, and provide counselors to speak with each kid individually. Guide counselors to use open-ended questions to allow kids to determine the direction of the conversation.

Encourage boys and girls to ask their parents, small group leaders, or other adults any questions they may have about becoming a Christian.

Key passage (5 minutes)

Leader • Has anyone memorized our key passage? These verses tell us about the believers in the early church. God blessed them, and the church grew.

Call on volunteers to recite the key passage from memory. Then display the key passage poster. Invite all the boys to read the key passage together, and then invite the girls.

Allow one or two volunteers to lead the class in singing "Every Day."

Discussion starter video (5 minutes)

Leader • Stephen was killed because he believed in Jesus, but even the threat of death did not cause Stephen to change his mind. Let's watch this video.

Show the "Unit 34 Session 3" video.

Leader • Have you ever been laughed at or made fun of because you go to church or read your Bible? Would you ever change your mind about Jesus because you didn't want to feel left out or embarrassed?

Tell them that in some countries, it is illegal to own a Bible or tell others about Jesus. Even today, Christians in many nations around the world face imprisonment or death for their faith in Jesus. They are not allowed to meet with other believers to worship God or read His Word.

Lead kids to discuss persecution and how it makes them feel. Direct kids to open their Bibles and read aloud Matthew 5:11-12.

Sing (3 minutes)

• "Build Your Kingdom Here" song

Leader • *Why was Stephen not afraid to die? Stephen saw Jesus waiting for him in heaven.* Stephen did not change his mind about what he believed. He laid down his life for the sake of Jesus and the church. Because of faithful believers and God's grace, the church is alive and growing today—more than two thousand years later! God is building His kingdom here through believers who are faithful to follow Jesus and tell others about Him no matter what. Let's sing!

Guide kids to sing together "Build Your Kingdom Here."

Prayer (2 minutes)

Leader • Before you go to small groups, let's pray.

Father God, we love You. We confess that we are not always bold for Your name. Sometimes we feel embarrassed to talk about Jesus. Lord, change us. Help us not to fear the world but to trust in You because You are in control. God, we pray for the believers all over the world who face persecution because they follow You. We pray You would give them comfort and strength. Guide them as they work to tell others about You.

You are worth any suffering we face in this life, and we look forward to the day we will be with You face to face. Amen.

Dismiss to small groups

The Gospel: God's Plan for Me

Ask kids if they have ever heard the word *gospel*. Clarify that the word *gospel* means "good news." It is the message about Christ, the kingdom of God, and salvation. Use the following guide to share the gospel with kids.

God rules. Explain to kids that the Bible tells us God created everything, and He is in charge of everything. Invite a volunteer to read Genesis 1:1 from the Bible. Read Revelation 4:11 or Colossians 1:16-17 aloud and explain what these verses mean.

We sinned. Tell kids that since the time of Adam and Eve, everyone has chosen to disobey God. (Romans 3:23) The Bible calls this sin. Because God is holy, God cannot be around sin. Sin separates us from God and deserves God's punishment of death. (Romans 6:23)

God provided. Choose a child to read John 3:16 aloud. Say that God sent His Son, Jesus, the perfect solution to our sin problem, to rescue us from the punishment we deserve. It's something we, as sinners, could never earn on our own. Jesus alone saves us. Read and explain Ephesians 2:8-9.

Jesus gives. Share with kids that Jesus lived a perfect life, died on the cross for our sins, and rose again. Because Jesus gave up His life for us, we can be welcomed into God's family for eternity. This is the best gift ever! Read Romans 5:8; 2 Corinthians 5:21; or 1 Peter 3:18.

We respond. Tell kids that they can respond to Jesus. Read Romans 10:9-10,13. Review these aspects of our response: Believe in your heart that Jesus alone saves you through what He's already done on the cross. Repent, turning from self and sin to Jesus. Tell God and others that your faith is in Jesus.

Offer to talk with any child who is interested in responding to Jesus.

Small Group LEADER

Session Title: Stephen's Address
Bible Passage: Acts 6:8–7:60
Big Picture Question: Why was Stephen not afraid to die? Stephen saw Jesus waiting for him in heaven.
Key Passage: Acts 2:42,47
Unit Christ Connection: The church is God's plan to bring praise and glory to Jesus.

Key passage activity (5 minutes)

- Key Passage Poster
- paper
- tape
- marker
- timer (optional)

Write the key passage on several pieces of paper, one word per page. Mix up the papers and tape them faceup to the floor. Display the key passage poster and guide kids to read it aloud. Then cover the poster and challenge kids to hop from page to page in order, saying the key passage aloud.

Kids may play one at a time or in a follow-the-leader style, hopping single-file through the key passage. If kids master the verse order, challenge them to hop through against a timer. See who can hop the passage the fastest!

Say • The believers in the early church devoted themselves to these things—the apostles' teaching, to fellowship, to eating meals together, and to praying.

• Stephen was a believer in the early church, and following the Lord was the most important thing in his life. He stood up for what he believed, even if it meant dying. *Why was Stephen not afraid to die? Stephen saw Jesus waiting for him in heaven.*

Bible story review & Bible skills (10 minutes)

- Bibles, 1 per kid
- Small Group Visual Pack

Give each kid a Bible and instruct boys and girls to find Acts 6. If kids need help, show them how to use the table of contents. Remind them that the Book of Acts comes after the four Gospels in the New Testament. Before asking review questions, you may choose to retell or review the Bible story using the bolded text of the Bible story script.

Ask each of the following review questions. Give kids a minute to search for the answer in the Bible. Kids should raise their hands when they find the answer. Then call on a kid to answer. If kids struggle, provide the verse reference.

1. Who gave Stephen wisdom when he spoke? (*the Holy Spirit, Acts 6:10*)
2. Where did the Jews take Stephen? (*to the Sanhedrin, or Jewish court; Acts 6:12*)
3. What part of the Bible did Stephen preach about? (*the Old Testament, Acts 7:2-50*)
4. What did Stephen accuse the Jewish leaders of doing? (*rejecting Jesus, the Messiah, and murdering Him; Acts 7:52*)
5. Whom did Stephen say he saw in heaven? (*Jesus standing at the right hand of God, Acts 7:55-56*)
6. What did the Jewish people do to Stephen? (*threw him out of the city and threw stones at him, Acts 7:58*)
7. What did Stephen ask the Lord to do? (*to receive his spirit and not to hold his murderers' sin against them, Acts 7:59-60*)

Say • Great job, everyone! Can you answer our big picture question? **Why was Stephen not afraid to die? Stephen saw Jesus waiting for him in heaven.**

• Stephen was killed because he was a Christian. Jesus told His followers that they would be persecuted—hated, hurt, or even killed—for loving Him. Jesus also said that those who suffer for Him would be blessed. (Matthew 5:11) We are going to face suffering in this life, but remember that Jesus suffered first. He died on the cross to take away our sins, and He rose from the dead. No matter what happens, we know that Jesus is waiting for us in heaven.

If you choose to review with boys and girls how to become a Christian, explain that kids are welcome to speak with you or another teacher if they have questions.

- **God rules.** God created and is in charge of everything. (Gen. 1:1; Rev. 4:11; Col. 1:16-17)
- **We sinned.** Since Adam and Eve, everyone has chosen to disobey God. (Rom. 3:23; 6:23)
- **God provided.** God sent His Son, Jesus, to rescue us from the punishment we deserve. (John 3:16; Eph. 2:8-9)
- **Jesus gives.** Jesus lived a perfect life, died on the cross for our sins, and rose again so we can be welcomed into God's family. (Rom. 5:8; 2 Cor. 5:21; 1 Pet. 3:18)
- **We respond.** Believe that Jesus alone saves you. Repent. Tell God that your faith is in Jesus. (Rom. 10:9-10,13)

Activity choice (10 minutes)

Option 1: You lose, you win

Guide kids to form pairs. Instruct the pairs to play a game of rock-paper-scissors, but play with a twist: the player in each pair who loses gets to keep playing. Each losing player pairs with another. Winning players will sit out. Play until only one player is left. (The player who loses most wins.)

Say • Even today, people who do not like Jesus often do not like His followers either. If you are mistreated or hurt for loving Jesus, you can be happy because you know you will be with Him forever. You might feel like you are losing, but with Jesus you will gain everything!

Option 2: Bible story poem

• pieces of paper, 5
• marker

Write each verse of the following Bible story poem on a separate piece of paper. Form five groups. If your group is small, kids may work individually or in pairs. Assign a verse to each group and instruct them to practice acting out their part of the Bible story.

After several minutes, invite each group to act out its portion for the rest of the group. Before each group performs, narrate the scene by reading the verse aloud.

(1) Stephen, a man full of wisdom and grace,
    When seized by the Jews, kept an angelic face.
(2) He preached of promises God had fulfilled
    And of the Messiah they rejected and killed.
(3) Their hearts filled with rage. They hated him so.
    They killed him with stones, but was he scared? No!
(4) For there in the heavens, he saw Christ his King:
    the reason he'd suffered, the reason he'd sing.
(5) "Forgive them!" he cried before dying that day.
    And then into heaven, his soul went to stay.

Say • *Why was Stephen not afraid to die? Stephen saw Jesus waiting for him in heaven.*

Journal and prayer (5 minutes)

• pencils
• journals
• Bibles
• Journal Page, 1 per kid (enhanced CD)
• "Following Jesus" activity page, 1 per kid

Distribute journals and journal pages. Encourage kids to write a prayer, asking God to take away any fear and to give them courage to stand up for His name.

As time allows, lead kids to complete the activity page "Following Jesus." Kids will use the key words listed to fill in the puzzle. Guide kids to count the number of spaces to determine where the key words fit. When kids finish, they should reveal the word *unafraid*. Review the Christ connection and remind kids that Stephen was not afraid to die because *Stephen saw Jesus waiting for him in heaven.*

Unit 35: PAUL'S CONVERSION AND MINISTRY

Big Picture Questions

Session 1:
How did Jesus change Saul's life? Jesus saved Saul from his sins.

Session 2:
What is a missionary? A missionary is someone who obeys God's call to go and tell others the good news about Jesus.

Session 3:
What did Paul do as he traveled? Paul started churches in other cities and taught people about Jesus.

Session 4:
Who deserves our worship? Only the Lord—the one true God—deserves our worship.

Session 5:
What did Paul tell people to do? Paul told people to turn from their sins and trust in Jesus.

Session 6:
How did God help Paul on his journey? God protected Paul so he could keep telling people about Jesus.

Unit 35: PAUL'S CONVERSION AND MINISTRY

Unit Description: God worked through Paul to bring the gospel to Rome, one of the most powerful and influential cities in the ancient world. Paul started churches and encouraged believers. Even though Paul was persecuted for his faith, he did not stop preaching about Jesus.

Unit Key Passage:
Romans 1:16

Unit Christ Connection:
God chose Paul to be a witness to all he had seen and heard of the risen Christ.

Session 1:
Paul's Conversion and Baptism
Acts 8:1-3; 9:1-31

Session 2:
Paul's First Journey
Acts 13:1–15:35

Session 3:
Paul's Second Journey
Acts 15:36–16:40

Session 4:
Paul Preached in Europe
Acts 17:1–18:21

Session 5:
Paul's Third Journey
Acts 18:18–21:16

Session 6:
Paul's Ministry to Rome
Acts 21:17–28:31

Leader BIBLE STUDY

Saul was no stranger to religion. He grew up in a religious household. He was a devout Jew who was born in Tarsus (Phil. 3:5) and inherited his Roman citizenship from his father. So when people began talking about this man named Jesus and claiming that He was the promised Messiah, Saul was defensive.

Saul believed strongly in the Jewish faith of his ancestors. He violently persecuted God's church and tried to destroy it. (Gal. 1:13-14) He dragged believers from their houses and put them in prison. He approved of the stoning of Stephen, the first Christian martyr. Saul thought he was doing the right thing by defending Judaism, but God's purposes could not be stopped.

As Saul was on his way to arrest believers in Damascus, the Lord stopped him in his tracks. Jesus revealed Himself to Saul, and Saul was never the same. He was struck blind and led into Damascus, where a believer named Ananias placed his hands on Saul. Suddenly, Saul could see again. Saul was convinced that Jesus is Lord. Saul later described the experience as being like dying and receiving a new life. (Gal. 2:20; 2 Cor. 5:17)

God had a purpose and a plan for Saul. He had set Saul apart before Saul was even born. (Gal. 1:15) God said, "This man is My chosen instrument to take My name to the Gentiles" (Acts 9:15).

Jesus changed Saul's life. As you teach kids, clarify that conversion happens when a person recognizes his sin, repents, believes in Jesus, and confesses Jesus as Savior and Lord. Jesus changes a person's heart, and as a result, his or her life is changed too.

Jesus appeared to Saul and changed him inside and out. Jesus Christ came into the world to save sinners. (1 Tim. 1:15) Jesus called Saul, who was once an enemy of Christians, to spend the rest of his life telling people the gospel and leading them to trust Jesus as Lord and Savior.

Older Kids BIBLE STUDY OVERVIEW

Session Title: Paul's Conversion and Baptism
Bible Passage: Acts 8:1-3; 9:1-31
Big Picture Question: How did Jesus change Saul's life? Jesus saved Saul from his sins.
Key Passage: Romans 1:16
Unit Christ Connection: God chose Paul to be a witness to all he had seen and heard of the risen Christ.

Additional suggestions for specific groups are available at *gospelproject.com/kids/additional-resources*.

For free online training on how to lead a group, visit *ministrygrid.com/web/thegospelproject*.

The BIBLE STORY

Paul's Conversion and Baptism
Acts 8:1-3; 9:1-31

When Stephen, a follower of Jesus, was killed for his faith, a man named Saul thought it was the right thing to do. At that time, the believers of the church in Jerusalem were being persecuted. **Saul wanted to put an end to the church.** He went into the houses of the people who believed in Jesus, dragged them out, and put them in jail. Many believers fled the city.

Saul headed to Damascus (duh MASS kuhs) **to arrest believers there. But on the way, a very bright light from heaven suddenly flashed around him. Saul fell to the ground. He heard a voice saying, "Saul, Saul, why are you persecuting Me?"**

"Who are You, Lord?" Saul asked.

"I am Jesus," He replied. "Get up and go into the city. Then you will be told what you must do."

Saul got up and opened his eyes, but he couldn't see! So the men who were traveling with Saul led him by the hand into Damascus.

A disciple of Jesus lived in Damascus. His name was Ananias (an uh NIGH uhs). **The Lord** spoke to Ananias in a vision. He **told him to go to the house where Saul was staying.** Ananias had heard of Saul. He knew that Saul had hurt many believers in Jerusalem and that he arrested anyone who believed in Jesus. But the Lord said, "Go! I have chosen this man to take My name to Gentiles, kings, and the Israelites."

Ananias obeyed the Lord. He found Saul and told Saul that Jesus had sent him to help Saul. **Ananias put his hands on Saul, and suddenly Saul could see again. Saul got up and was baptized.**

For the next few days, Saul stayed with the believers in Damascus. He began to go to the synagogues to preach about Jesus. Saul told the people, "Jesus is the Son of God!"

The people were amazed. They recognized Saul and knew he had wanted to put an end to the church and all the believers. Now he was one of them! **The Jews did not like Saul's message, so they planned to kill him. Saul heard what the Jews wanted to do, so one night he left the city.**

The disciples helped Saul escape by lowering him down the city wall in a basket.

Saul went to Jerusalem. He tried to join in with the other believers, but they did not trust him. They knew Saul had been an enemy of believers. How could he be their friend? But one believer, Barnabas, accepted Saul. He told the other apostles how God had changed Saul and how Saul had preached about Jesus in Damascus.

Saul stayed with the believers in Jerusalem. He spoke boldly for God. But the Jews in the city wanted to kill Saul, so the believers sent Saul away. Now the church was at peace. The group of believers became stronger, and more people joined the church. **Later, Saul became known by his Roman name, Paul.**

Christ Connection: Jesus appeared to Saul and changed him inside and out. Jesus Christ came into the world to save sinners. (1 Timothy 1:15) Jesus called Saul, also known as Paul, who was once an enemy to Christians, to spend the rest of his life telling people the gospel and leading them to trust Jesus as Lord and Savior.

Want to discover God's Word? Get *Bible Express*!
Invite kids to check out today's devotional to discover that the Lord's ways show His faithful love to those who love Him. (Psalm 25:10) Why did God blind Saul on the road to Damascus? Because God's plans for us are always bigger and better than we know! Order in bulk, subscribe quarterly, or purchase individually. For more information, check out *www.lifeway.com/devotionals*.

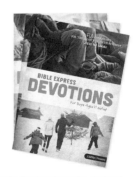

Small Group OPENING

Session Title: Paul's Conversion and Baptism
Bible Passage: Acts 8:1-3; 9:1-31
Big Picture Question: How did Jesus change Saul's life? Jesus saved Saul from his sins.
Key Passage: Romans 1:16
Unit Christ Connection: God chose Paul to be a witness to all he had seen and heard of the risen Christ.

Welcome time

Greet each kid as he or she arrives. Use this time to collect the offering, fill out attendance sheets, and help new kids connect to your group. Ask volunteers to share about big changes they have experienced (a move, birth of a sibling, parent job change, and so forth). Be sensitive to kids' responses; life changes can be difficult or stressful.

Activity page (5 minutes)

- "A Changed Man" activity page, 1 per kid
- pencils

Distribute activity pages and encourage kids to work in pairs. Explain that there are 10 differences between the two pictures. Can they find all 10? (*hair, eye color, glasses, teeth, beard, scarf, sleeves, belt, sandals, rock*)

Say • Things are changing all around us. Seasons change, weather changes, and even people change. Today we're going to learn about someone who changed.

Session starter (10 minutes)

- index cards
- marker

Option 1: Change your mind

Write several statements on index cards such as, *Baseball is the best sport* or *Green is the best color*. Choose a volunteer to read a card. If kids agree, they should stand. If they disagree, they should sit. Then challenge the volunteer to make an argument to convince kids who are sitting to stand. For example, if kids don't agree that pickles are the best food, the volunteer might describe them as crunchy and delicious, a perfect addition to a sandwich for lunch.

Encourage kids to be creative. After a few minutes, allow another volunteer to try to change other kids' minds.

Say •You might change your opinion about your favorite color or pizza topping, but you might need a lot more convincing the change your mind about a fact. Today's Bible story is about a man who changed his mind when he learned the truth about Jesus.

Option 2: Blindfolded building

• blindfolds, 1 per kid
• rope or string

Instruct kids to pick a leader. Then arrange the kids in a straight row and place a rope at their feet. Make sure the rope is long enough for everyone to hold with both hands.

Help each kid put on a blindfold or tell him to keep his eyes closed. Give the following instructions:

1. Pick up the rope at your feet.
2. No one is allowed to talk, but the appointed leader may ask three questions while you work.
3. Form a square (or circle, rectangle, or so forth).
4. When the group is finished, everyone should drop the rope at their feet.

Guide the kids to remove their blindfolds and examine their shape. Play again to form other shapes as time allows.

Say •Today we are going to hear a story from the Bible about a man who suddenly couldn't see. Something happened to him, and it changed his life!

Transition to large group

Large Group LEADER

Session Title: Paul's Conversion and Baptism
Bible Passage: Acts 8:1-3; 9:1-31
Big Picture Question: How did Jesus change Saul's life? Jesus saved Saul from his sins.
Key Passage: Romans 1:16
Unit Christ Connection: God chose Paul to be a witness to all he had seen and heard of the risen Christ.

• room decorations

Tip: Select decorations that fit your ministry and budget.

Suggested Theme Decorating Ideas: Simulate an RV campground by arranging a few lawn chairs at the front of the room. Set up a small table with a checkered tablecloth. You may wish to create a backdrop of an RV on a large sheet of paper or bedsheet. Display other props such as a mountain bike, camping supplies, and electric lanterns.

Countdown

• countdown video

Show the countdown video as your kids arrive, and set it to end as large group time begins.

Introduce the session (3 minutes)

• leader attire
• sunglasses
• map or road atlas

[Large Group Leader enters carrying a road atlas and wearing sunglasses on the top of his or her head. Leader is tracing a path on the map with his or her finger, humming.]

Leader • Hello, everyone! You're here! What perfect timing. I am just getting ready to leave for a five-week road trip, but I have to make some last minute adjustments. [*Point to map.*] You see, I was planning on going from here to this town over here, but not long after I got on the road this morning, all the traffic just stopped. It turns out that the road is closed because of some sort of accident. Rumor has it that a pedestrian was walking along when he had some kind of medical emergency. He is going to be OK, but the paramedics had to come and take him to the next town for treatment.

Anyway, I was turning around to find another route when I hit a pothole and blew a tire. So now I'm just waiting for a mechanic to change the tire so I can get back on the road. You all are welcome to join me! I'm excited for this road trip because as I travel, I'm learning all about a man from the Bible named Paul. Let me tell you more.

Timeline map (1 minute)

• Timeline Map

Leader • You see, this is our timeline map. It's kind of like a road map, but it shows some events from the Bible and when they happened. The first stop on our adventure is right here. Hey, I know him! Well, we've never met because he lived a long time ago, but this is Paul! Today's Bible story is about some things that happened to Paul. These were big events that changed Paul's life.

Big picture question (1 minute)

Leader • Raise your hand if you are a good listener. Oh, perfect! I have a task for you. As you listen to the Bible story, will you pay close attention and see if you can hear the answer to our big picture question? The question is, *How did Jesus change Saul's life?* Here we go!

Tell the Bible story (10 minutes)

• "Paul's Conversion and Baptism" video
• Bibles, 1 per kid
• Bible Story Picture Slide or Poster
• Big Picture Question Slide or Poster

Open your Bible to Acts 9:1-31. Tell the Bible story in your own words, or show the Bible story video "Paul's Conversion and Baptism."

Leader • Let me give you some background information about Paul. When he was born, his parents named him

Tip: A Bible story script is provided at the beginning of every session. You may use it to guide you as you prepare to teach the Bible story in your own words. For a shorter version of the Bible story, read only the bolded text.

Saul, which is a Hebrew name. But since his dad was a Roman citizen, they gave him another name too: Paul. Paul is a Latin name. So Saul and Paul are names for the same person. He is most commonly known as Paul.

Saul grew up in a religious family. He was a Jew, and he followed the law very carefully. So when Saul heard people say that a man named Jesus was the Messiah, he did not believe it. In fact, he tried to stop people from telling others about Jesus. He arrested believers and even approved of them being killed, like when the Jews killed Stephen. He tried to put an end to the early church.

Saul was on his way to arrest believers in the city of Damascus when Jesus stopped him on the road. Saul saw a bright light from heaven and heard a voice. He said, "Who are you, Lord?" and Jesus said, "I am Jesus."

After that, Saul knew that Jesus is Lord. Saul went into the city and a believer named Ananias came and touched Saul, and Saul could see again. Then he was baptized.

Saul wasn't the same after that. This story describes his *conversion*, or his change from one belief to another. Saul changed because he believed that Jesus is God's Son. Then Saul was baptized to show that he believed in Jesus as Savior and Lord.

How did Jesus change Saul's life? Jesus saved Saul from his sins. Can you say that with me? ***How did Jesus change Saul's life? Jesus saved Saul from his sins.***

Jesus came to save sinners. Saul was a sinner, and you and I are sinners. Before God changes us, we might not think about Jesus at all. Or maybe like Saul, we don't want anything to do with Jesus.

What do you think about Jesus? Have you heard the good news?

The Gospel: God's Plan for Me (optional)

Using Scripture and the guide provided, explain to boys and girls how to become a Christian. Tell kids how they can respond, and provide counselors to speak with each kid individually. Guide counselors to use open-ended questions to allow kids to determine the direction of the conversation.

Encourage boys and girls to ask their parents, small group leaders, or other adults any questions they may have about becoming a Christian.

Key passage (5 minutes)

- Key Passage Slide or Poster
- "I'm Not Ashamed" song

Leader • Everyone who met Saul after his experience on the road to Damascus was amazed at how he had changed. But Saul didn't change himself; the Lord changed him!

Show the key passage poster and read it aloud. Then lead the kids to read it aloud a couple of times.

Leader • These words were written by Paul. The good news about Jesus, the gospel, is powerful. By believing it, people are saved from their sins. God wants everyone to hear this good news. Long ago, he saved Paul so that Paul would tell the gospel to the whole world—to both Jews and non-Jews (Greeks or Gentiles). Let's sing.

Guide boys and girls in singing "I'm Not Ashamed."

Discussion starter video (4 minutes)

- "Unit 35 Session 1" discussion starter video

Leader • Do you think Paul went home from Damascus and continued to arrest believers? No! Paul was a changed man after he believed in Jesus. Watch this video.

Show the "Unit 35 Session 1" video.

Leader • When Jesus saves you, He changes you inside and out. Instead of you being the most important person in your life, Jesus is most important.

Lead kids to discuss how a person might act before she believes in Jesus, and how she might act after she trusts Jesus as Lord and Savior.

Sing (4 minutes)

• "Shake" song

Leader •*How did Jesus change Saul's life? Jesus saved Saul from his sins.* When God saves someone, that person is changed. The Bible says that when someone believes in Jesus, he is a new creation. That doesn't mean a person suddenly stops sinning, but the Holy Spirit is working to make that person like Jesus.

Explain that the theme song is about being changed. Invite boys and girls to sing it together.

Prayer (2 minutes)

Leader •Thank you for joining me today! That tire on my RV should be changed by now, so I better get going. Before you go to your small groups, let's pray.

Lead kids in prayer. Thank God for sending Jesus to save sinners. Pray that kids would understand and believe the gospel and that Jesus would change them inside and out.

Dismiss to small groups

The Gospel: God's Plan for Me

Ask kids if they have ever heard the word *gospel*. Clarify that the word *gospel* means "good news." It is the message about Christ, the kingdom of God, and salvation. Use the following guide to share the gospel with kids.

God rules. Explain to kids that the Bible tells us God created everything, and He is in charge of everything. Invite a volunteer to read Genesis 1:1 from the Bible. Read Revelation 4:11 or Colossians 1:16-17 aloud and explain what these verses mean.

We sinned. Tell kids that since the time of Adam and Eve, everyone has chosen to disobey God. (Romans 3:23) The Bible calls this sin. Because God is holy, God cannot be around sin. Sin separates us from God and deserves God's punishment of death. (Romans 6:23)

God provided. Choose a child to read John 3:16 aloud. Say that God sent His Son, Jesus, the perfect solution to our sin problem, to rescue us from the punishment we deserve. It's something we, as sinners, could never earn on our own. Jesus alone saves us. Read and explain Ephesians 2:8-9.

Jesus gives. Share with kids that Jesus lived a perfect life, died on the cross for our sins, and rose again. Because Jesus gave up His life for us, we can be welcomed into God's family for eternity. This is the best gift ever! Read Romans 5:8; 2 Corinthians 5:21; or 1 Peter 3:18.

We respond. Tell kids that they can respond to Jesus. Read Romans 10:9-10,13. Review these aspects of our response: Believe in your heart that Jesus alone saves you through what He's already done on the cross. Repent, turning from self and sin to Jesus. Tell God and others that your faith is in Jesus.

Offer to talk with any child who is interested in responding to Jesus.

Small Group LEADER

Session Title: Paul's Conversion and Baptism
Bible Passage: Acts 8:1-3; 9:1-31
Big Picture Question: How did Jesus change Saul's life? Jesus saved Saul from his sins.
Key Passage: Romans 1:16
Unit Christ Connection: God chose Paul to be a witness to all he had seen and heard of the risen Christ.

Key passage activity (5 minutes)

• Key Passage Poster

Display the key passage poster and lead kids to read the verse aloud. Form a group of boys and a group of girls. Instruct boys to read two words and then girls to read two words. Groups should read back and forth until they've said the verse and reference.

Choose six key words or phrases and assign to each group. Allow kids to make up motions for the key words and present them to the group. Then say the key passage together, using the motions.

Bible story review & Bible skills (10 minutes)

• Bibles, 1 per kid
• Small Group Visual Pack

Option: Retell or review the Bible story using the bolded text of the Bible story script.

Say • In what book of the Bible can you find our Bible story? (*Acts*) Who wrote the Book of Acts? (*Luke*) What does the Book of Acts tell us about? (*the early church*) Invite all of the kids to stand. Challenge them to listen closely as you review the Bible story.

Kids should turn 45 degrees to the left when they hear the word *left*, and 45 degrees to the right when they hear the word *right*. Read the following script:

• Saul wanted to stop the church. He marched *right* into the houses of believers and dragged them off to jail. Many believers *left*. Then Saul *left* and went to Damascus. On the way, a bright light flashed before Saul, and he fell *right* to the ground. Jesus talked to Saul and Saul realized that Jesus is Lord, and to attack believers is not *right*!

- Saul got up, but he could not see. In Damascus, a believer named Ananias *left* his house to find Saul. He put his hands on Saul—his *right* hand and his *left* hand—and Saul could see again. Saul went to the synagogue to teach people what he knew is *right*: Jesus is the Son of God!

- The people did not like Saul's message, so Saul *left* and went back to Jerusalem. He went to live with the other believers, but they did not accept him *right* away. But Barnabas accepted Saul and told the others how Saul had *left* his old way of living. Now the church was growing, and Saul became known by his other name, Paul.

Say • *How did Jesus change Saul's life? Jesus saved Saul from his sins.*

If you choose to review with boys and girls how to become a Christian, explain that kids are welcome to speak with you or another teacher if they have questions.

- **God rules.** God created and is in charge of everything. (Gen. 1:1; Rev. 4:11; Col. 1:16-17)

- **We sinned.** Since Adam and Eve, everyone has chosen to disobey God. (Rom. 3:23; 6:23)

- **God provided.** God sent His Son, Jesus, to rescue us from the punishment we deserve. (John 3:16; Eph. 2:8-9)

- **Jesus gives.** Jesus lived a perfect life, died on the cross for our sins, and rose again so we can be welcomed into God's family. (Rom. 5:8; 2 Cor. 5:21; 1 Pet. 3:18)

- **We respond.** Believe that Jesus alone saves you. Repent. Tell God that your faith is in Jesus. (Rom. 10:9-10,13)

Activity choice (10 minutes)

Option 1: What's different?

Invite kids to play a game. Lead each kid to find a partner. Direct partners to stand facing each other. If you have an odd number of kids, let an adult partner with a child.

Instruct each child to look carefully at his partner for 30 seconds. Encourage him to study every detail about his partner's clothing, hair, and appearance. Then tell each pair to turn back-to-back. Guide each child to change one thing about his appearance that can be clearly seen.

If kids need help with ideas, offer these suggestions:

1. Untie a shoe.
2. Change a hairstyle.
3. Roll up a sleeve.
4. Remove glasses.
5. Pull out a pocket.
6. Remove jewelry.
7. Roll down a sock.
8. Turn up a collar.

Challenge kids to turn around and see which partner can first identify what's different. Allow kids to switch partners and play again.

Say • After Saul met Jesus, he was changed! Saul went from arresting believers and throwing them in prison to going into the synagogues to tell people that Jesus is the Son of God! Everyone who saw Saul was amazed at the change.

• When Jesus saves someone, He changes that person from His enemy into His friend.

Option 2: Change matters

- water and ice
- popcorn and kernel
- raw egg and fried egg
- fresh bread and toast
- oranges and orange juice

Display the object pairs on a table at the front of the room. Start with the first pair, water and ice. Ask kids to raise their hands if they can tell what the difference is between the water and the ice. Call on a kid to explain.

As you point out each set of objects, talk about the types of physical or chemical changes. How did each object change? How did cooking or heating or squeezing change one object into another form?

Say • When Jesus changed Saul, He changed Saul spiritually. Saul's sins had separated him from God, but when Saul trusted in Jesus, God forgave his sins and gave Saul eternal life.

• *How did Jesus change Saul's life? Jesus saved Saul from his sins.*

Journal and prayer (5 minutes)

- pencils
- journals
- Bibles
- Journal Page, 1 per kid (enhanced CD)
- "Changed! Word Ladder" activity page, 1 per kid

Distribute journals and journal pages. Encourage kids to draw a picture of Saul before he encountered Jesus and a picture of him after he met Jesus.

Say • *How did Jesus change Saul's life? Jesus saved Saul from his sins.*

As time allows, lead kids to complete the activity page "Changed! Word Ladder." Kids will start at the top of the ladder and work their way down, using the clues to fill in the blanks. (*Saul, sail, fail, fall, hall, haul, Paul*)

Review the Christ connection and remind kids that Jesus changed Saul. Saul became known as Paul, and he spent the rest of his life telling people the good news about Jesus. People who trust in Jesus as Lord and Savior are changed!

Leader BIBLE STUDY

Paul's first missionary journey began in Antioch of Syria—the third-largest city in the Roman empire, after Rome and Alexandria. Antioch was about 20 miles inland from the Mediterranean Sea and nearly 300 miles north of Jerusalem. The Holy Spirit was working in the Antioch church. The Spirit led the believers there to send out Paul and Barnabas on a journey to preach. The church obeyed, and Paul and Barnabas went out.

Now Paul—the man who had devotedly persecuted Christians—was a missionary. A missionary is someone who obeys God's call to go and tell others the good news about Jesus. Paul and Barnabas traveled to several cities and all over the island of Cyprus, telling everyone about Jesus.

In each city, they went first into the synagogues. They told the Jews about Jesus. Some of them believed, but some of them were angry at Paul and Barnabas. They rejected the truth about Jesus. In some places, the Jews made plans to kill Paul!

Paul and Barnabas faced a lot of trouble because they told people about Jesus. So Paul and Barnabas went to the Gentiles, the non-Jews. This was the purpose to which God had called Paul. (See Acts 9:15.) When the Gentiles heard the gospel, many of them believed.

Help kids understand the meaning of the word *Gentile*. Gentiles are people who are not Jews. The gospel is not for a select group of people; it is for everyone! If Paul had not taken the gospel to the Gentiles, many of us would probably not be believers today.

Paul obeyed the Holy Spirit's call to tell the world about Jesus. Many of the Jews rejected Christ, so Paul shared the gospel with the non-Jews. Many of them believed in Jesus. God uses people to tell others about Jesus so that people all over the world can be saved from their sin by trusting in Jesus as Lord and Savior.

Older Kids BIBLE STUDY OVERVIEW

Session Title: Paul's First Journey

Bible Passage: Acts 13:1–15:35

Big Picture Question: What is a missionary? A missionary is someone who obeys God's call to go and tell others the good news about Jesus.

Key Passage: Romans 1:16

Unit Christ Connection: God chose Paul to be a witness to all he had seen and heard of the risen Christ.

Small Group Opening

Large Group Leader

Small Group Leader

Additional suggestions for specific groups are available at *gospelproject.com/kids/additional-resources*.

For free online training on how to lead a group, visit *ministrygrid.com/web/thegospelproject*.

The BIBLE STORY

Paul's First Journey
Acts 13:1–15:35

Paul and his friend **Barnabas were with the church in Antioch. The Holy Spirit chose Paul and Barnabas for a special work.** So they obeyed and left Antioch to do the work.

First, Paul and Barnabas sailed to the island of Cyprus (SIGH pruhs). **They stopped in different cities and taught the good news about Jesus** in the Jewish synagogues. **Some people believed the message they were telling. Next, Paul and Barnabas** traveled back to the mainland. **They went to the city of Antioch in Asia.** On the Sabbath Day, Paul and Barnabas went to the synagogue. The people invited them to speak, so **Paul began to preach the message of Jesus.**

Paul explained that people can be forgiven for their sins through Jesus. He said that believing in Jesus is the only way to be forgiven. **Keeping the Law of Moses cannot free someone from sin.** He urged the Jewish listeners to believe what he was saying. **When Paul and Barnabas got ready to leave, the people asked them to come back** on the next Sabbath Day. They wanted to know more.

So the next week, Paul and Barnabas went back to the synagogue. It was crowded! Not only had the Jews returned, but **almost everyone in the city—Jews and Gentiles** (non-Jews)**—had come to hear the message of Jesus. The Jews** saw all the people, and they **were jealous. They argued with Paul and Barnabas and shouted at them.**

"We told God's message to the Jews first," Paul said, "but you refuse to listen!" God had a plan to use Paul as a light for other nations—for Gentiles too. Paul would reach people all over the world and show them how to be saved. This was happy news for the Gentiles, and many of them believed the message of God. But **the Jews** were against Paul and Barnabas and **kicked them out of the city.**

Next, Paul and Barnabas went to the city of Iconium (igh KOH nih uhm). **The same thing happened there!** They spoke in the synagogue, and **many Jews and Greeks believed the message about Jesus. But the Jews who refused to believe stirred up trouble.** They planned to kill Paul and

Barnabas, but **Paul and Barnabas** escaped.

They **traveled to Lystra** (LISS truh), **and Paul healed a man there who was lame. The people** saw what Paul had done, and they **thought Paul and Barnabas were gods!** They began to praise them, but **Paul and Barnabas shouted, "No! We are not gods. We are men just like you! We want to tell you the good news of God."**

Then some people showed up from Antioch and Iconium. They caused trouble so that the people in Lystra turned against Paul and Barnabas too. They threw stones at Paul and dragged him out of the city. They thought he was dead, but the believers in Lystra **gathered around Paul, and he got up.**

The next day, Paul and Barnabas went to the city of Derbe (DUHR bih). **They told people there about Jesus, and many people believed.** Then they went back to Lystra and to Iconium. They encouraged the believers there to continue in the faith.

Finally, Paul and Barnabas returned to the church at Antioch. They reported everything God had done on their journey and how God had helped them share the good news with the Gentiles.

Christ Connection: Paul obeyed the Holy Spirit's call to tell the world about Jesus. Many of the Jews rejected Christ, so Paul shared the gospel with the non-Jews. Many of them believed in Jesus. God uses people to tell others about Jesus so that people all over the world can be saved from their sin by trusting in Jesus as Lord and Savior.

Want to discover God's Word? Get *Bible Express*!

Invite kids to check out today's devotional to discover why it is so important to study the Bible— the Scriptures help us understand how to be forgiven of our sins. (2 Timothy 3:15) Paul taught the Jews and non-Jews from Scriptures that salvation is found in Jesus Christ alone. Order in bulk, subscribe quarterly, or purchase individually. For more information, check out *www.lifeway.com/devotionals*.

Small Group OPENING

Session Title: Paul's First Journey
Bible Passage: Acts 13:1–15:35
Big Picture Question: What is a missionary? A missionary is someone who obeys God's call to go and tell others the good news about Jesus.
Key Passage: Romans 1:16
Unit Christ Connection: God chose Paul to be a witness to all he had seen and heard of the risen Christ.

Welcome time

Greet each kid as he or she arrives. Use this time to collect the offering, fill out attendance sheets, and help new kids connect to your group.

As kids arrive, invite them to share about trips they have taken. Have they ever traveled out of the state? Or out of the country? Where did they go and what did they do?

Activity page (5 minutes)

• "Nation or Not?" activity page, 1 per kid
• pencils

Give boys and girls the "Nation or Not?" activity page and instruct them to mark whether or not they think each nation listed actually exists. After a couple of minutes, ask kids to share their guesses.

Say • Have you heard of all of these places? Well, all of these nations listed are actual nations! They really exist! Did you know that there are billions of people in the world? Many of them have never even heard about Jesus.

• Today we are going to hear a story from the Bible about a man whose job was to lead people from other nations to trust in Jesus as Lord and Savior.

Session starter (10 minutes)

Option 1: Cars zoom!

Instruct kids to stand. Randomly select a leader. The leader will stand in front of the class and say, "Cars zoom!" All the kids should move their hands as if they are holding a steering wheel and say "Zoom!"

The leader will continue to call out modes of transportation by saying, for example, "Trains zoom," or "Bikes zoom." As long as the leader calls out a mode of transportation, the children will say, "Zoom!"

If the leader names something that is not used for travel, kids should remain quiet. Kids who say "Zoom!" must sit. Choose a new leader after three or four things are called.

Say • Today's Bible story is about someone who traveled a lot. He didn't travel by car or plane or train, though. Sometimes he walked and sometimes he sailed in ships. I wonder where he traveled.

Option 2: Sketch it out

- "Missionary Jobs" (enhanced CD)
- paper
- markers

Stack the cards facedown. Call kids one at a time to be the artist. The artist must draw a card and then illustrate the person or object on the card. Kids should try to guess what the player is drawing.

Allow kids to review the drawings and match any related items and people. (*doctor, stethoscope; photographer, camera; pilot, airplane*; and so forth)

Say • All of these tools are things that can be used by missionaries, and all of these jobs are jobs that missionaries might do. Today we are going to learn about someone in the Bible who was a missionary.

Transition to large group

Large Group LEADER

Session Title: Paul's First Journey
Bible Passage: Acts 13:1–15:35
Big Picture Question: What is a missionary? A missionary is someone who obeys God's call to go and tell others the good news about Jesus.
Key Passage: Romans 1:16
Unit Christ Connection: God chose Paul to be a witness to all he had seen and heard of the risen Christ.

Countdown

• countdown video

Show the countdown video as your kids arrive, and set it to end as large group time begins.

Introduce the session (3 minutes)

• leader attire
• sunglasses
• car keys

[Large Group Leader enters carrying a set of car keys and wearing sunglasses on the top of his or her head. Leader jingles the keys.]

Leader • Hello! Welcome back, everyone. I am just packing up because it is time to hit the road! The bags are packed, the maps are folded, the tire is changed, and my sunglasses are safely tucked away right here … *[Begin patting pants or jacket pockets as if you can't find your sunglasses.]* Oh no! Has anyone seen my sunglasses? *[Reach on top of your head.]* Ah! Here they are!

I've got several places I want to stop today. I hope you like tourist traps! If you're ready to go, sit back and relax like you're in a spacious RV. I'd like to take this opportunity to remind you to keep your arms and legs inside the vehicle at all times. Always wear your seat belt, and remember, this vehicle stops at all railroad crossings!

Timeline map (2 minutes)

• Timeline Map

Leader • Can anyone tell me what we learned last time? Here's the picture of this man on the ground. Who is this? (*Saul or Paul*) Right! Saul was an enemy of Jesus, but Jesus changed him and then Saul wanted to tell everyone about Jesus! Saul had another name, Paul. That's what we will call him now. Today's Bible story is called "Paul's First Journey." This picture here shows two guys who look a bit upset. Everyone else seems to love them, though. I wonder what's going on.

Big picture question (1 minute)

Leader • We will soon find out what this story is all about. As you listen, see if you can figure out the answer to our big picture question: ***What is a missionary?*** I'll give you a hint: Paul was a missionary. Now check this out.

Tell the Bible story (10 minutes)

• "Paul's First Journey" video
• Bibles, 1 per kid
• Bible Story Picture Slide or Poster
• Big Picture Question Slide or Poster
• "Paul's First Journey Map" (enhanced CD)

Open your Bible to Acts 13 and tell the Bible story in your own words, or show the Bible story video "Paul's First Journey."

Leader • Paul was ready to go after Jesus changed him! Paul and Barnabas were at the church in Antioch. Think of that as kind of their "home base." [*Show the map of Paul's first journey and point out the key locations.*] The Holy Spirit called Paul and Barnabas to go and tell people about Jesus. They left Antioch and went to the island of Cyprus. Then they went to a city in Asia that was also called Antioch. From there, Paul and Barnabas went to Iconium (igh KOH nih uhm), Lystra (LISS truh), and Derbe (DUHR bih) before they went back home.

At each place, Paul and Barnabas went into the synagogues to talk to the Jews. They told the people that the only way to be forgiven of sin is to trust in Jesus as Lord and Savior. Paul said that no one could be saved by keeping the law; no one is good enough to save themselves.

Some of the people who listened to Paul believed what he was saying, but many of the Jews did not like this message. Since the Jews would not listen, Paul preached the gospel to the Gentiles, or non-Jews. This made the Jews angry, and they ran Paul and Barnabas out of town.

Paul faced trouble in every city, but he did not quit the job God gave him to do. Paul was a missionary. We can look at his life and answer our big picture question: *What is a missionary?* Do you know the answer? *A missionary is someone who obeys God's call to go and tell others the good news about Jesus.* Let's practice that.

Guide boys and girls to say the big picture answer. Provide a few words and then pause for them to fill in the blanks:

"*A missionary is someone who <u>obeys</u> God's call to <u>go</u> and <u>tell others</u> the <u>good news</u> about <u>Jesus</u>.*"

Leader • God used Paul for His work, and He uses people today to tell others about Jesus so that people all over the world can be saved from their sin by trusting in Jesus as Lord and Savior.

The Gospel: God's Plan for Me (optional)

Using Scripture and the guide provided, explain to boys and girls how to become a Christian. Tell kids how they can respond, and provide counselors to speak with each kid individually. Guide counselors to use open-ended questions to allow kids to determine the direction of the conversation.

Encourage boys and girls to ask their parents, small group leaders, or other adults any questions they may have about becoming a Christian.

Key passage (5 minutes)

• Key Passage Slide or Poster
• "I'm Not Ashamed" song

Display the key passage poster. Read it aloud, teaching kids motions for the key words or phrases to help them remember the verse. Consider these suggested motions:

- *I am not ashamed*—stand tall and shake your head
- *it is God's*—point upward
- *power*—flex arms
- *to everyone*—point to everyone
- *who believes*—point to head
- *first to the Jew*—hold up one finger
- *and also to the Greek*—hold up two fingers

Leader • Paul wrote these words. He obeyed God's call to go and tell others the good news about Jesus. Jesus died on the cross to take away our sins, and He is alive!

Paul was not embarrassed by the gospel, and when the Jews would not listen, he told the good news to the Greeks. Greeks are people who live in Greece; they were not Jews. Paul believed that the gospel is for everyone!

Lead the group in singing the song "I'm Not Ashamed."

Discussion starter video (4 minutes)

• "Unit 35 Session 2" discussion starter video

Leader • What would you do if your teacher at school said that recess was going to last all day? Or that there would be no more homework? Or that your favorite singer was coming to visit? Would you keep it to yourself? No! Check out this video.

Show the "Unit 35 Session 2" video. Then lead kids to discuss why they might share good news with others.

Leader • Good news travels fast! God sent Paul to share the gospel, the good news about Jesus, with the whole world. God wants us to share this good news too. Who can you tell about Jesus?

Sing (4 minutes)

• "Shake" song

Leader •Once Paul believed in Jesus, he could not sit still! Paul was changed, and he had to tell others the good news. Have you been changed like Paul? Let's shake!

Play the song "Shake" and lead kids to sing along.

Prayer (1 minute)

Leader •Great job, everyone. Before you go to small groups, I'm going to pray.

Lord, thank You for sending Jesus to save us from our sins. We know that we can never be good enough to earn salvation, so we put our trust in Jesus, who never sinned. This good news is for everyone! Help us to not be ashamed or embarrassed to tell others about You. We love You, Father. Amen.

Dismiss to small groups

The Gospel: God's Plan for Me

Ask kids if they have ever heard the word *gospel*. Clarify that the word *gospel* means "good news." It is the message about Christ, the kingdom of God, and salvation. Use the following guide to share the gospel with kids.

God rules. Explain to kids that the Bible tells us God created everything, and He is in charge of everything. Invite a volunteer to read Genesis 1:1 from the Bible. Read Revelation 4:11 or Colossians 1:16-17 aloud and explain what these verses mean.

We sinned. Tell kids that since the time of Adam and Eve, everyone has chosen to disobey God. (Romans 3:23) The Bible calls this sin. Because God is holy, God cannot be around sin. Sin separates us from God and deserves God's punishment of death. (Romans 6:23)

God provided. Choose a child to read John 3:16 aloud. Say that God sent His Son, Jesus, the perfect solution to our sin problem, to rescue us from the punishment we deserve. It's something we, as sinners, could never earn on our own. Jesus alone saves us. Read and explain Ephesians 2:8-9.

Jesus gives. Share with kids that Jesus lived a perfect life, died on the cross for our sins, and rose again. Because Jesus gave up His life for us, we can be welcomed into God's family for eternity. This is the best gift ever! Read Romans 5:8; 2 Corinthians 5:21; or 1 Peter 3:18.

We respond. Tell kids that they can respond to Jesus. Read Romans 10:9-10,13. Review these aspects of our response: Believe in your heart that Jesus alone saves you through what He's already done on the cross. Repent, turning from self and sin to Jesus. Tell God and others that your faith is in Jesus.

Offer to talk with any child who is interested in responding to Jesus.

Small Group LEADER

Session Title: Paul's First Journey
Bible Passage: Acts 13:1–15:35
Big Picture Question: What is a missionary? A missionary is someone who obeys God's call to go and tell others the good news about Jesus.
Key Passage: Romans 1:16
Unit Christ Connection: God chose Paul to be a witness to all he had seen and heard of the risen Christ.

Key passage activity (5 minutes)

- Key Passage Poster
- toy cars
- adhesive labels
- marker

Write each word of the key passage on a separate label and label each toy car. Distribute the cars to kids and challenge them to arrange the cars in the correct order.

When kids finish, guide them to check their work against the key passage poster. Then say the key passage together. If time allows, mix up the cars and play again.

Say • Can anyone tell me who wrote these words? (*Paul*)
   • Paul was not ashamed of the gospel. He was happy to share the good news about Jesus with others. Paul knew that when people hear the gospel, some of them will believe in Jesus and be saved.

Bible story review & Bible skills (10 minutes)

- Bibles, 1 per kid
- Small Group Visual Pack
- red paper plates, 1 per kid
- green paper plates, 1 per kid

Consider retelling or reviewing the Bible story using the bolded text of the Bible story script.

Give each kid a red plate and a green plate. Explain that the red plate stands for "false" and the green plate stands for "true." Read the following statements and invite kids to respond by holding up their "true" or "false" plates.

1. Paul traveled with his friend Barnabas. (*true, Acts 13:2-3*)

2. Paul taught that people can be forgiven of their sin by living good lives. (*false, Acts 13:38-39*)
3. Paul said that people are forgiven only by believing in Jesus. (*true, Acts 13:38*)
4. Paul preached the gospel to both the Jews and Gentiles, or non-Jews. (*true, Acts 13:46*)
5. Everyone who listened to Paul's message accepted it and believed in Jesus. (*false, Acts 13:45-46*)
6. All of the Jews welcomed Paul and invited him to stay as long as he wanted. (*false, Acts 13:50; 14:19*)
7. The people in Lystra thought Paul and Barnabas were gods. (*true, Acts 14:11*)
8. Paul was a missionary. (*true*)

Say • *What is a missionary? A missionary is someone who obeys God's call to go and tell others the good news about Jesus.*

If you choose to review with boys and girls how to become a Christian, explain that kids are welcome to speak with you or another teacher if they have questions.

- **God rules.** God created and is in charge of everything. (Gen. 1:1; Rev. 4:11; Col. 1:16-17)
- **We sinned.** Since Adam and Eve, everyone has chosen to disobey God. (Rom. 3:23; 6:23)
- **God provided.** God sent His Son, Jesus, to rescue us from the punishment we deserve. (John 3:16; Eph. 2:8-9)
- **Jesus gives.** Jesus lived a perfect life, died on the cross for our sins, and rose again so we can be welcomed into God's family. (Rom. 5:8; 2 Cor. 5:21; 1 Pet. 3:18)
- **We respond.** Believe that Jesus alone saves you. Repent. Tell God that your faith is in Jesus. (Rom. 10:9-10,13)

Activity choice (10 minutes)

Option 1: Find a place

Tell everyone to find a place to stand in the room. Kids should be at least an arm's length away from each other. Give the following instructions:

1. This is your "first place." Try to memorize where you are standing.
2. Now find another place to stand. This is your "second place." Remember where you are standing now.
3. Move to a third place, and then a fourth, and then a fifth place. Remember each spot!
4. Let's review. Everyone return to your first place. Now move to your second, third, fourth, and fifth places.
5. At my signal, go to your next place by moving in the way I call out. (*jumping, walking, skipping, walking backward, twirling, waddling like a penguin*, and so forth)

For an added challenge, instead of calling out numbers, call out the names of the places Paul visited on his first journey. Kids should move between the places in order. (*1: Cyprus, 2: Antioch, 3: Iconium, 4: Lystra, 5: Derbe*)

Say • Paul traveled to five places on his first journey: Cyprus, Antioch, Iconium, Lystra, and Derbe. Paul was a missionary. ***What is a missionary? A missionary is someone who obeys God's call to go and tell others the good news about Jesus.***

Option 2: Magnetic maps

- poster board
- art supplies
- paper clips
- magnetic buttons or craft magnets

Provide a piece of poster board for groups of three or four kids. Encourage each group to use art supplies to decorate the poster board like a map.

Kids may illustrate places in their own neighborhoods or create their own communities. Instruct kids to draw and label at least five specific locations on the map. Then provide paper clips and magnets. Demonstrate how to hold the magnetic against the underside of the poster to move the paper clip around the map.

Invite kids to "travel" from each of the places they drew. As kids create and play, talk about all the places Paul went on his first journey. Remind kids that Paul obeyed God's call to go and tell others the good news about Jesus.

Say • Paul was a missionary. *What is a missionary? A missionary is someone who obeys God's call to go and tell others the good news about Jesus.*

Journal and prayer (5 minutes)

- pencils
- journals
- Bibles
- Journal Page, 1 per kid (enhanced CD)
- "What Is a Missionary?" activity page, 1 per kid

Distribute journal pages and suggest kids

Say • Paul told everyone—Jews and non-Jews—about Jesus. The gospel is for everyone, not just a special group of people. This is good news because that means anyone who trusts in Jesus is forgiven for his or her sins. Let's pray.

Pray, thanking God for making the way for all people—people from every nation—to be part of God's family. Thank Him for calling Paul to be a missionary. Now, two thousand years later, we hear and believe the gospel because of the faithful believers before us.

As time allows, lead kids to complete the activity page "What Is a Missionary?" Encourage kids to use the key to decipher the secret message.

When kids finish, ask them to share the answer. (*A missionary is someone who obeys God's call to go and tell others the good news about Jesus.*)

Leader BIBLE STUDY

As Paul traveled, he started churches in other cities and taught people about Jesus. Paul's second journey took him from Antioch in Syria back to some of the cities he visited on his first journey. Paul wanted to see how the new believers were doing. From Antioch, Paul and his companion Silas traveled through Syria and Cilicia, encouraging believers and strengthening churches. The numbers of believers in the churches increased daily.

One night, while Paul and Silas were in Troas, the Lord called Paul to go to Macedonia and preach the gospel to the people. So Paul and Silas obeyed. They sailed to Macedonia, staying in the city of Philippi for several days.

Two major events happened while Paul was in Macedonia. First, a woman named Lydia became a believer. Paul and Silas had gone to the river to pray. They spoke to the women at the river. God opened Lydia's heart to the good news of the gospel. She believed and was baptized. Then she invited Paul and Silas to stay at her house.

Then, a jailer became a believer. This happened when Paul and Silas were thrown into prison after Paul commanded a fortune-telling spirit to come out of a slave girl. Late at night, an earthquake rocked the prison. The prisoners could have jumped up and escaped, but they stayed where they were. The jailer asked Paul and Silas how to be saved. "Believe in the Lord Jesus, and you will be saved," they said. The man believed and was baptized.

Emphasize the Christ connection as you review the Bible story with kids: Lydia was saved and the jailer was saved because they believed in Jesus. Jesus offers us salvation as a gift. He did all the work to save us by dying on the cross. We do not need to earn salvation; we can receive it by repenting and trusting in Jesus.

Older Kids BIBLE STUDY OVERVIEW

Session Title: Paul's Second Journey
Bible Passage: Acts 15:36–16:40
Big Picture Question: What did Paul do as he traveled? Paul started churches in other cities and taught people about Jesus.
Key Passage: Romans 1:16
Unit Christ Connection: God chose Paul to be a witness to all he had seen and heard of the risen Christ.

Small Group Opening

Large Group Leader

Small Group Leader

Additional suggestions for specific groups are available at *gospelproject.com/kids/additional-resources*.

For free online training on how to lead a group, visit *ministrygrid.com/web/thegospelproject*.

The BIBLE STORY

Paul's Second Journey
Acts 15:36–16:40

Paul had traveled to several towns with Barnabas, and they shared the good news about Jesus. Many people believed their message, but others were against them and did not believe. A few days after Paul and Barnabas arrived back in Antioch, Paul decided to go back to the towns. He wanted to check on the new believers and see how they were doing. This time, Paul chose Silas (SIGH luhs) to go with him. Silas was a leader in the early church. So the church sent them out. **Paul and Silas traveled through the countries of Syria and Cilicia** (sih LISH ih uh). **They met with the churches there. All the churches were getting stronger, and more people believed in Jesus every day.**

One night, Paul saw a vision. A vision is like a dream, but Paul was awake. **In the vision, God told Paul to go to Macedonia** (MASS uh DOH nih uh). **God wanted Paul to share the gospel with the people there.**

So Paul and his companions went to Macedonia. They stopped for a few days in a city called Philippi (FIH lih pigh). **On the Sabbath Day, Paul and his friends went outside the city to the river to pray. Some women were there, and Paul started talking to them. A woman named Lydia was listening, and God opened her heart to accept what Paul was saying. Lydia and everyone in her house was baptized.**

On another day, Paul and Silas were on their way to pray, and **a servant girl met them. She had a spirit in her that allowed her to predict the future.** She earned a lot of money for her masters by telling the future. **The girl followed Paul and Silas, shouting, "These men,** who are telling you how to be saved, **are servants of the Most High God!"** She followed them for many days. **Finally, Paul turned and said to the spirit in her, "By the power of Jesus Christ, I command you to come out of her!" And the spirit came out right away.**

Now the girl's owners were upset because she could no longer tell the future and make money for them. They grabbed Paul and Silas and dragged them to the authorities. They complained about the things Paul and Silas were doing. **The officials ordered for Paul and Silas to be**

Older Kids Bible Study Leader Guide
Unit 35 • Session 3

beaten and thrown into jail.

About midnight, Paul and Silas were praying and singing songs to God. The other prisoners were listening to them. **All of a sudden, a violent earthquake shook the foundation of the jail. All the doors flew open, and everyone's chains came loose! The jailer woke up and saw the prison doors open. He thought the prisoners had escaped, so he took out his sword and was about to kill himself.**

"Don't hurt yourself!" Paul said. "We are all here!"

The jailer rushed inside and fell down in front of Paul and Silas, shaking with fear. Then he **took Paul and Silas outside. "Men, what must I do to be saved?" he asked.**

They said to him, "Believe in the Lord Jesus and you will be saved—you and your household." Paul and Silas told the message of Jesus to the jailer and to everyone in his household. All of them believed and were baptized right away.

The jailer washed Paul's and Silas' wounds. He brought them into his house and fed them. Later that day, Paul and Silas were set free.

Christ Connection: Lydia, the jailer, and many others were saved because they believed in Jesus. Jesus offers us salvation as a gift. He did all the work to save us by dying on the cross. We do not need to earn salvation; we can just receive it by repenting and trusting in Jesus.

Want to discover God's Word? Get *Bible Express*!

Invite kids to check out today's devotional to discover that, just as God took care of Paul and Silas when they were imprisoned, God will supply all our needs in Christ Jesus. (Philippians 4:19) We can joyfully pray to God and trust Him to take care of us! Order in bulk, subscribe quarterly, or purchase individually. For more information, check out *www.lifeway.com/devotionals.*

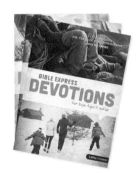

Small Group OPENING

Session Title: Paul's Second Journey
Bible Passage: Acts 15:36–16:40
Big Picture Question: What did Paul do as he traveled? Paul started churches in other cities and taught people about Jesus.
Key Passage: Romans 1:16
Unit Christ Connection: God chose Paul to be a witness to all he had seen and heard of the risen Christ.

Welcome time

Greet each kid as he or she arrives. Use this time to collect the offering, fill out attendance sheets, and help new kids connect to your group.

Activity page (5 minutes)

• "A-Maze-ing Journey" activity page, 1 per kid
• pencils

Give boys and girls the "A-Maze-ing Journey" activity page. Instruct them to find the correct path through the maze to discover where Paul went on his second journey. (*Macedonia*)

Say • Paul traveled to many places, and he shared with many people the good news about Jesus. Today we are going to hear about Paul's second journey.

Session starter (10 minutes)

• classroom furniture
• cardboard boxes (optional)
• timer (optional)

Option 1: Earthquake obstacle course
Use available classroom furniture to arrange a simple obstacle course. Turn over chairs and position tables on their sides. You may choose to use cardboard boxes as additional obstacles for kids to move through or around.

Instruct kids how to safely move through the course. Point out areas where they should move over, under, or around certain obstacles. Then lead kids to take turns moving through the course. Encourage them to cheer for each other or race against a timer.

Say • It looks like there was an earthquake in here! Today we are going to hear a story about a time Paul experienced a real earthquake.

Option 2: Dye paper purple

Cut tissue paper into 8½-by-11-inch rectangles. Provide one piece per kid. Pour purple liquid watercolor paint into small cups. Take the following steps to create purple paper:

1. Accordion fold the tissue paper back and forth into 1-inch widths to form a long strip.
2. Fold the lower left corner toward the opposite edge of the paper to form a triangle. The right side of the triangle should line up with the right side of the vertical strip.
3. Turn over the paper and fold the triangle straight up to create a thicker triangle. Continue to press and fold until you reach the top of the strip. Wrap a rubber band around the corners to hold the triangle together.
4. Dip each point of the triangle into the paint for 1 or 2 seconds. Kids may wish to leave the center of the triangle undyed.
5. Take off the rubber band and unwrap the triangle very carefully. The wet tissue paper may tear easily. Lay the paper flat to dry.

Say • In today's Bible story, Paul shared the gospel with a woman named Lydia who sold purple cloth. The dye required to make purple cloth was very expensive.

Transition to large group

- white tissue paper
- rubber bands
- purple liquid watercolor paint
- small cups
- scissors

Tip: Work on a vinyl tablecloth and keep paper towels handy for easy cleanup.

Large Group LEADER

Session Title: Paul's Second Journey
Bible Passage: Acts 15:36–16:40
Big Picture Question: What did Paul do as he traveled? Paul started churches in other cities and taught people about Jesus.
Key Passage: Romans 1:16
Unit Christ Connection: God chose Paul to be a witness to all he had seen and heard of the risen Christ.

Countdown

• countdown video

Show the countdown video as your kids arrive, and set it to end as large group time begins.

Introduce the session (3 minutes)

• leader attire
• cloth bag
• various toys, games, or books

[Large Group Leader enters carrying a cloth bag full of various toys, games, or books suitable for a road trip.]

Leader • Hi, everyone! Are you ready to embark on the second leg of our trip? We'll be on the road most of the day today, so I brought a bag of toys and games and books to read. Do any of you like to play games or sing songs or tell stories when you travel?

We are going to do all of those things today. Sit back and relax as the RV gets moving. Let's imagine we are cruising through the countryside while I tell you about today's Bible story.

Timeline map (2 minutes)

• Timeline Map

Leader • First, let's take a look at the map. Here is where we started a couple weeks ago. We learned about Saul, who started going by the name Paul after he believed in Jesus. Then we learned about the first journey Paul took.

Paul and Barnabas traveled to several cities to tell people about Jesus.

Today we are going to hear about Paul's second journey. Let's see … here is the Bible story picture. Paul is sitting, talking to some women by a river. I wonder whom Paul told about Jesus this time.

Big picture question (1 minute)

Leader • As you listen to the Bible story, see if you can figure out the answer to our big picture question, *What did Paul do as he traveled?* Well, he probably didn't play games like these! [*Hold up cloth bag of games.*]

Tell the Bible story (10 minutes)

- "Paul's Second Journey" video
- Bibles, 1 per kid
- Bible Story Picture Slide or Poster
- Big Picture Question Slide or Poster
- "Paul's Second Journey Map" (enhanced CD)

Open your Bible to Acts 15 and tell the Bible story in your own words, or show the Bible story video "Paul's Second Journey." As you review the Bible story, point to the locations on the map of Paul's second journey.

Leader • *What did Paul do as he traveled? Paul started churches in other cities and taught people about Jesus.*

On his second journey, Paul left Antioch in Syria and visited some of the places he went on his first journey— Derbe, Lystra, Iconium, and Antioch in Asia. In each city, Paul met with the believers and encouraged them to keep following Jesus. Every day, more people believed in Jesus and the church grew.

Then Paul and his friend Silas went to the city of Troas (TROH az). While they were there, Paul had a vision. He saw a man who begged Paul to come to Macedonia to help the people there. Paul understood the vision was from God, so he decided to go to Macedonia.

Paul and Silas stopped in the city of Philippi. One day, the went to the river to pray. Paul started talking to some women at the river. One of the women was named Lydia. God opened her heart to accept what Paul was saying. Lydia believed in Jesus. Lydia was baptized, and so was everyone in her household.

On another day, a servant girl started following Paul and Silas. She had a spirit in her, and she earned money for her owners by telling the future. When she followed Paul and Silas, she started shouting things like, "These men are servants of God!" Paul commanded the spirit to come out of her, and the spirit did. Now the girl's owners were upset because she could no longer tell the future and make them money. So they had Paul and Silas arrested and thrown into jail.

While they were in jail, Paul and Silas prayed and sang songs to God. They could have escaped from jail when an earthquake caused all the doors to open, but they did not. They told the jailer about Jesus. The jailer was baptized, and so was everyone in his household.

Let's review our big picture question. Did you hear the answer? *What did Paul do as he traveled? Paul started churches in other cities and taught people about Jesus.*

Did Lydia or the jailer have to do anything to be saved? Did they have to do a certain number of good deeds or give a large amount of money for God to accept them? No! Salvation is a gift from God that we can have by believing in Jesus. We do not need to earn salvation; we can receive it by turning away from our sins and trusting in Jesus.

The Gospel: God's Plan for Me (optional)

Read Acts 16:31 from today's Bible story. Using Scripture and the guide provided, explain to boys and girls how to become a Christian. Tell kids how they can respond, and provide counselors to speak with each kid individually. Guide counselors to use open-ended questions to allow kids to determine the direction of the conversation.

Encourage boys and girls to ask their parents, small group leaders, or other adults any questions they may have about becoming a Christian.

Key passage (5 minutes)

• Key Passage Slide or Poster
• "I'm Not Ashamed" song

Leader •Did you catch the answer to our big picture question? ***What did Paul do as he traveled? Paul started churches in other cities and taught people about Jesus.*** Paul was not afraid or embarrassed to tell people about Jesus. The gospel is good news!

Show the key passage poster and lead the group in reading it aloud. Challenge volunteers who have memorized Romans 1:16 to say it from memory. Then invite boys and girls to sing "I'm Not Ashamed."

Discussion starter video (4 minutes)

Leader •Are you unashamed of the gospel like Paul was? Would anything stop you from telling others about Jesus? Think about that as you watch this.

• "Unit 35 Session 3" discussion starter video

Show the "Unit 35 Session 3" video.

Leader •Would you tell about Jesus if it meant traveling to a foreign country? Or going to jail?

Lead kids to discuss some of the persecution Paul faced and how they would respond today.

Sing (3 minutes)

• "Shake" song

Leader •Paul was serious about following Jesus. Paul was completely changed after he trusted in Jesus. He couldn't sit still; he had to share the good news of the gospel! Have you been changed too? Let's sing and shake!

Invite kids to move around and "shake" as they sing the unit theme song.

Prayer (2 minutes)

Leader • Thank you, everyone, for joining me today. Let's pray before you go to your small groups.

Lead kids in prayer. Praise God for sending His Son, Jesus, to save us from our sins. Thank Him for the church and for giving believers the honor of sharing the good news about Jesus with the whole world.

Pray that kids would trust in Jesus alone for their salvation and that they would stay faithful in the face of suffering or persecution.

Dismiss to small groups

The Gospel: God's Plan for Me

Ask kids if they have ever heard the word *gospel*. Clarify that the word *gospel* means "good news." It is the message about Christ, the kingdom of God, and salvation. Use the following guide to share the gospel with kids.

God rules. Explain to kids that the Bible tells us God created everything, and He is in charge of everything. Invite a volunteer to read Genesis 1:1 from the Bible. Read Revelation 4:11 or Colossians 1:16-17 aloud and explain what these verses mean.

We sinned. Tell kids that since the time of Adam and Eve, everyone has chosen to disobey God. (Romans 3:23) The Bible calls this sin. Because God is holy, God cannot be around sin. Sin separates us from God and deserves God's punishment of death. (Romans 6:23)

God provided. Choose a child to read John 3:16 aloud. Say that God sent His Son, Jesus, the perfect solution to our sin problem, to rescue us from the punishment we deserve. It's something we, as sinners, could never earn on our own. Jesus alone saves us. Read and explain Ephesians 2:8-9.

Jesus gives. Share with kids that Jesus lived a perfect life, died on the cross for our sins, and rose again. Because Jesus gave up His life for us, we can be welcomed into God's family for eternity. This is the best gift ever! Read Romans 5:8; 2 Corinthians 5:21; or 1 Peter 3:18.

We respond. Tell kids that they can respond to Jesus. Read Romans 10:9-10,13. Review these aspects of our response: Believe in your heart that Jesus alone saves you through what He's already done on the cross. Repent, turning from self and sin to Jesus. Tell God and others that your faith is in Jesus.

Offer to talk with any child who is interested in responding to Jesus.

Small Group LEADER

Session Title: Paul's Second Journey
Bible Passage: Acts 15:36–16:40
Big Picture Question: What did Paul do as he traveled? Paul started churches in other cities and taught people about Jesus.
Key Passage: Romans 1:16
Unit Christ Connection: God chose Paul to be a witness to all he had seen and heard of the risen Christ.

Key passage activity (5 minutes)

- Key Passage Poster
- permanent marker
- masking tape
- large plastic building blocks

Use a permanent marker to write the words of the key passage on separate pieces of masking tape. Include a piece of tape for the key passage reference.

Stick each word onto a large plastic building block and mix up the blocks. Allow kids to sort and arrange the blocks so the key passage is in the correct order. Guide them to read the verse aloud. Challenge kids to put the verse in order by laying out a long train, building a tall tower, or constructing a block wall.

Say • Good work! Think about this verse anytime you feel unsure about telling someone about Jesus.

Bible story review & Bible skills (10 minutes)

- Bibles, 1 per kid
- Small Group Visual Pack
- index cards
- marker

Option: Retell or review the Bible story using the bolded text of the Bible story script.

Write the following passages on separate index cards: *Acts 16:13-15; Acts 16:16-24;* and *Acts 16:25-33.*

Provide a Bible for each kid. Guide boys and girls to find the Book of Acts in the Bible. Assist any kids who need help. Ask which Bible books come before the Book of Acts. (*the Gospels: Matthew, Mark, Luke, and John*)

Form three groups. Give each group an index card. Instruct kids to find their assigned passages in the Bible and prepare a short skit to act out the scene. Give kids several minutes to prepare, and then call on each group to present three of the major events from Paul's second journey. After each group performs, ask a few review questions:

Acts 16:13-15

1. Why did Paul and Silas go to the river? (*to pray, Acts 16:13*)
2. What was the name of the woman at the river? (*Lydia, Acts 16:14*)
3. What happened to Lydia and her household? (*They were baptized, Acts 16:15*)

Acts 16:16-24

1. How did the servant girl make money for her owners? (*by telling the future, Acts 16:16*)
2. What did the servant girl say about Paul and Silas? (*"These men are servants of the Most High God!" Acts 16:17*)
3. What did the girl's owners do to Paul and Silas? (*dragged them to the authorities, Acts 16:19*)

Acts 16:25-33

1. What were Paul and Silas doing while in prison? (*praying and singing to God, Acts 16:25*)
2. What caused the prison doors to open and the prisoners' chains to come loose? (*an earthquake, Acts 16:26*)
3. What did Paul and Silas say the jailer needed to do to be saved? (*"Believe in the Lord Jesus," Acts 16:31*)

Say • Lydia, the jailer, and many others were saved because they believed in Jesus. Jesus offers us salvation as a gift. He did all the work to save us by dying on the cross. We do not need to earn salvation; we can just receive it by repenting and trusting in Jesus.

If you choose to review with boys and girls how to become

a Christian, explain that kids are welcome to speak with you or another teacher if they have questions.

- **God rules.** God created and is in charge of everything. (Gen. 1:1; Rev. 4:11; Col. 1:16-17)
- **We sinned.** Since Adam and Eve, everyone has chosen to disobey God. (Rom. 3:23; 6:23)
- **God provided.** God sent His Son, Jesus, to rescue us from the punishment we deserve. (John 3:16; Eph. 2:8-9)
- **Jesus gives.** Jesus lived a perfect life, died on the cross for our sins, and rose again so we can be welcomed into God's family. (Rom. 5:8; 2 Cor. 5:21; 1 Pet. 3:18)
- **We respond.** Believe that Jesus alone saves you. Repent. Tell God that your faith is in Jesus. (Rom. 10:9-10,13)

Activity choice (10 minutes)

• large playground ball

Option 1: Bridge ball

Instruct kids to stand in a circle, foot to foot. Their legs should be slightly more than shoulder-width apart, forming a "bridge." Direct the kids to get ready to play by putting their hands on their knees.

Explain that the goal of the game is to hit the ball between another player's legs and to keep the ball from going between your own legs. Players should hit the ball with an open palm, and the ball must stay on the ground. Players may not reach in front of others to get the ball.

If the ball goes between a player's legs, pause play and guide everyone to say the big picture question and answer together: *What did Paul do as he traveled? Paul started churches in other cities and taught people about Jesus.*
Say • Where did Paul go on his second journey?

(Macedonia, the city of Philippi; Acts 16:10-12)
- Who believed in Jesus? *(Lydia, the jailer, and both of their households; Acts 16:14-15,29-30,33-34)*

Option 2: Exponential growth

- dry pasta noodles or other small manipulatives

Clear a large surface for kids to arrange manipulatives, such as pasta noodles. Position a single noodle at one end of the work area. Explain that this noodle represents one person. Then position two more noodles a few inches from the first and a few inches apart. Tell kids to imagine that the first person told two others about Jesus.

Note: The number of manipulatives will double in each row. To illustrate the growth of the early church, imagine the number of believers doubled each generation.

For each second person, position two more noodles so that you have four more noodles evenly spaced. Tell kids that each of those two people told two more people. Now four more people believed in Jesus! Allow kids to continue adding rows of noodles, two new noodles per one previous noodle. Show how the number of noodles grows; the tenth row would have 512 noodles, and then twentieth: 524,288!

Say • God blessed the early church and the work of Paul and other missionaries like him. More and more people believed in Jesus, and the church grew.

- *What did Paul do as he traveled? Paul started churches in other cities and taught people about Jesus.*

Journal and prayer (5 minutes)

- pencils
- journals
- Bibles
- Journal Page, 1 per kid (enhanced CD)
- Gospel Plan Poster (enhanced CD)
- "Earthquake!" activity page, 1 per kid

Distribute journal pages and encourage kids to write prayers, thanking Jesus for the free gift of salvation.

As time allows, lead kids to complete the activity page "Earthquake!" Distribute copies of the Gospel Plan Poster. Review the gospel as kids match each symbol to the corresponding statement. *(God rules, crown; We sinned, X; God provided, cross; Jesus gives, gift; We respond, hands)*

Leader BIBLE STUDY

Paul and Silas traveled to Thessalonica and began preaching in the synagogue about Jesus. Some became believers, but others wanted to attack them. Paul and Silas escaped and went to Berea. The Jews in Berea studied the Scriptures to make sure Paul was telling the truth. Many of them believed! But when the Jews in Thessalonica heard what was happening in Berea, they hurried there and caused trouble. So Paul went to Athens.

The city of Athens was a cultural center. People in Athens loved to hear about and study the latest ideas. Paul spoke with the Jews and the philosophers in the city. Athens was also full of idols to every kind of god. There was even an altar to an unknown god.

4 Paul began preaching, telling the people that they worshiped a god they did not know. But people can know the Lord God! He made the world and everything in it! God was not like their idols. "We ought not to think that God is like gold or silver or stone, an image formed by the art and imagination of man," Paul said.

Paul told the people that God wanted them to turn away from their sins. Then Paul told them about Jesus and how He was raised from the dead. Some people made fun of Paul, but others believed.

From Athens, Paul went to Corinth. He tried to persuade the Jews in the synagogue that Jesus is the Christ, but they would not listen. Paul spoke to the Gentiles, and many of them believed and were baptized. God continued working through Paul.

The men of Athens worshiped many false gods. Paul explained to them God's plan of salvation. He said that only God should be worshiped. Paul talked about Jesus and the resurrection. People can know God because Jesus took the punishment for sin that separates people from God. Only the Lord—the one true God—deserves our worship.

Older Kids BIBLE STUDY OVERVIEW

Session Title: Paul Preached in Europe
Bible Passage: Acts 17:1–18:21
Big Picture Question: Who deserves our worship? Only the Lord—the one true God—deserves our worship.
Key Passage: Romans 1:16
Unit Christ Connection: God chose Paul to be a witness to all he had seen and heard of the risen Christ.

Additional suggestions for specific groups are available at *gospelproject.com/kids/additional-resources*.

For free online training on how to lead a group, visit *ministrygrid.com/web/thegospelproject*.

U N I T

35

4

The BIBLE STORY

Paul Preached in Europe
Acts 17:1–18:21

Paul and Silas were in Macedonia when they **came to the city of Thessalonica** (THESS uh loh NIGH kuh). **Paul went into the synagogue to meet with the Jews**, as he always did. For three weeks, on each Sabbath Day, **Paul talked with them about the Scriptures. Paul said, "This Jesus I am telling you about is the Messiah." Some of the Jews believed Paul and Silas, and they decided to join them.**

But the Jews who did not believe were jealous. They formed a mob and started a riot in the city. They went to the home of Paul's friend Jason, looking for Paul and Silas. They were not there, so the mob dragged Jason and some of the other believers to the city leaders. "They say there is another king—Jesus!" the mob shouted. The city leaders were upset. They made Jason and the other believers pay money, and then they let them go.

That night, Paul and Silas went to another city called Berea (buh REE uh). **The people there listened to Paul's message, and they studied the Scriptures to make sure he was telling them the truth. Many people in Berea believed the good news.** But the Jews in Thessalonica heard what Paul was up to in Berea. They followed him there and caused trouble, so **Paul left and went to the city of Athens in Greece.**

Paul was upset by what he saw in Athens. The people there did not worship the one true God. Instead, they worshiped many idols. Paul talked with the people who lived in Athens and told them the good news about Jesus and the resurrection.

The men asked Paul to explain what he was talking about. So Paul went to a meeting with them and said, "Men of Athens, I can see that you are very religious. I saw in your city an altar that said: 'TO AN UNKNOWN GOD.' You worship a god that you do not know. This is the God I want to tell you about."

So **Paul told the people about the one true God. He explained that God made everything**, and that He is bigger than man-made temples. **God is not like the idols in Athens.** He is not made of gold, silver, or stone. **Paul said that God wants everyone in the world to turn away from** their sin and turn to Him.

When the people heard about Jesus being raised from the dead, some of them laughed. Some of them wanted to hear more later. Some of them joined Paul and became believers.

Later, Paul left Athens and went to the city of Corinth. There he met a Jewish man named Aquila (uh KWIL uh) and his wife, Priscilla. They were tentmakers, and so was Paul, so Paul stayed with them and worked with them. On the Sabbath Days, Paul went to the synagogues to preach.

Paul stayed in Corinth for a year and a half, teaching God's message to the people. Then Paul left to go back to Antioch.

Christ Connection: The men of Athens worshiped a false god whom they did not know. Paul explained to the men God's plan of salvation. He said that only God should be worshiped. Paul talked about Jesus and the resurrection. People can know God because Jesus took the punishment for sin that separates people from God.

Want to discover God's Word? Get *Bible Express*!

Invite kids to check out today's devotional to discover what was difficult for the people of Athens to understand. God—who made the universe and everything in it—chose to send His only Son to die on the cross and rise again, so we could be forgiven of our sins! (John 3:16) Order in bulk, subscribe quarterly, or purchase individually. For more information, check out *www.lifeway.com/devotionals*.

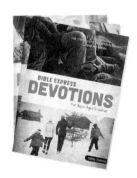

Small Group OPENING

Session Title: Paul Preached in Europe
Bible Passage: Acts 17:1–18:21
Big Picture Question: Who deserves our worship? Only the Lord—the one true God—deserves our worship.
Key Passage: Romans 1:16
Unit Christ Connection: God chose Paul to be a witness to all he had seen and heard of the risen Christ.

Welcome time

Greet each kid as he or she arrives. Use this time to collect the offering, fill out attendance sheets, and help new kids connect to your group. Ask kids to tell about their favorite toy or game. Where did they get it? Why is it their favorite?

Activity page (5 minutes)

• "Where Was Paul?" activity page, 1 per kid
• pencils

Distribute the "Where Was Paul?" activity page. Instruct kids to read the clues and use the process of elimination to determine which city Paul was in.

Say • In today's Bible story, Paul went on another journey. Where was Paul? (*Athens*)

Session starter (10 minutes)

Option 1: Guess what

Invite the kids to play a guessing game. Start by exclaiming, "I see something … " and then use adjectives to describe the object you see. For example: "I see something green." Allow kids to guess what you see.

When a kid guesses correctly, allow him a turn to choose an object. He should whisper to you what he has chosen and then describe it for the group. Play several rounds.

Say • In today's Bible story, Paul looked around a city and saw the people worshiping many different idols. But Paul taught them that they should not worship things that are created by people.

• I see … that it's time to go to large group! Let's go!

Option 2: Silent message

• bandanas or other small objects, 2
• coin

Form two equal teams. Instruct each team to stand in a single-file line. Team members should hold hands and face the other team. Guide the first person in each line—the leader—to stand at the front of the room. Position a bandana on the ground at the end of each line. Explain how to play the game.

1. When you begin, all the players should close their eyes and keep quiet.
2. Flip a coin. Only the leaders in each line may watch to see if it lands on heads or tails. If the coin lands on tails, flip again.
3. If the coin lands on heads, the leaders should return to their lines and squeeze the first player's hand.
4. The players at the front of the line should send the squeeze down the line.
5. When the squeeze reaches the last player in line, he or she should try to pick up the bandana first.

After each round, the last player becomes the leader. Play several rounds.

Say • Paul had a message to share, and he could not keep quiet! He traveled to many different cities to tell people about it. Let's get ready to learn more.

Transition to large group

Large Group LEADER

Session Title: Paul Preached in Europe
Bible Passage: Acts 17:1–18:21
Big Picture Question: Who deserves our worship? Only the Lord—the one true God—deserves our worship.
Key Passage: Romans 1:16
Unit Christ Connection: God chose Paul to be a witness to all he had seen and heard of the risen Christ.

Countdown

• countdown video

Show the countdown video as your kids arrive, and set it to end as large group time begins.

Introduce the session (2 minutes)

• leader attire
• family-size cooler
• snacks and bottled water (optional)

[Large Group Leader enters dragging a large cooler. Leader may choose to pack the cooler with bottled water and snacks. Pull the cooler slowly and with great effort as if it is very heavy. Park the cooler and sit on it.]

Leader •Ugh! Whew! My goodness. This is a heavy cooler. It is very important, though, because it is full of snacks and drinks for the road! Have you ever been on a long road trip and been hungry or thirsty? Sometimes it is hard to wait to get to your destination! I like to pack snacks and drinks so we don't have to stop and buy some.

What are some of your favorite things to eat or drink on a road trip? *[Allow kids to respond.]* Yes, I like those things too. Say, are you ready to get started? Let's go.

Timeline map (2 minutes)

• Timeline Map

Point out the Bible story pictures from previous weeks.
Leader •Let's check out our timeline map.

After Paul believed in Jesus, he started traveling to many different cities, telling people the good news of the gospel. Paul was a missionary. **What is a missionary? A missionary is someone who obeys God's call to go and tell others the good news about Jesus.**

Next, Paul went on a second journey. This time he went with his friend Silas. They traveled to Macedonia and stopped in the city of Philippi. **What did Paul do as he traveled? Paul started churches in other cities and taught people about Jesus.**

Here is today's Bible story picture. It looks like Paul is speaking to a group of people, but these people don't look very sure about what Paul is saying.

Big picture question (1 minute)

Leader • Our big picture question might help us figure out why these people look unsure. Today's big picture question is, **Who deserves our worship?** Hmm … that is a very big question and a very important one! Let's find out. Listen carefully.

Tell the Bible story (10 minutes)

• "Paul Preached in Europe" video
• Bibles
• Bible Story Picture Slide or Poster
• Big Picture Question Slide or Poster
• "Paul's Journey in Europe Map" (enhanced CD)

Open your Bible to Acts 17 and tell the Bible story in your own words, or show the Bible story video "Paul Preached in Europe." As you review the Bible story, show the map tracing Paul's journey in Europe. Point out the key places: Philippi, Thessalonica, Berea, Athens, and Corinth.

Leader • Paul's time in Europe started out like a lot of his other visits to new places. Paul started out in Philippi, and he went to Thessalonica. He went to the synagogue where Jews went to worship God, and he told people there that Jesus is God's Son. Did the Jews believe him? Some of them did, but many did not. Those who didn't believe were angry, and they caused trouble for Paul.

Next, Paul went to Berea (buh REE uh). What did the people in Berea do when they listened to Paul? That's right! They looked in the Scriptures to make sure Paul was telling the truth. Remember, the Bible is God's Word. Everything in it is true. When we aren't sure if something someone says about God is right, we can go to the Bible.

After Berea, Paul went to Athens. Athens was a very important city in Paul's day. The people in Athens loved to hear new ideas and think deep thoughts. But the people did not worship the one true God. What did Paul see when he went to Athens? He saw that the city was full of idols! The people created things out of gold or silver or stone, and they worshiped them as if they were gods.

This made Paul upset! Nothing created by human hands deserves to be worshiped. ***Only the Lord—the one true God—deserves our worship.*** That's the answer to our big picture question. ***Who deserves our worship? Only the Lord—the one true God—deserves our worship.***

Paul taught the people that God wanted them to turn away from their sins. He told them about Jesus, who died on a cross and then came alive again. Some people believed, but some people laughed at Paul!

Finally, Paul went to Corinth. He talked to the Jews there, but they did not believe what he said about Jesus. So Paul talked to the Gentiles, people who were not Jews. Many of them believed and were baptized.

OK. So the people in Athens worshiped idols. They worshiped false gods they did not know! Our sin separates us from God, but Jesus died on the cross to take away our sin. When we trust in Him as Lord and Savior, we can know God—the one true God. Only He deserves our worship.

The Gospel: God's Plan for Me (optional)

• Bible

Using Scripture and the guide provided, explain to boys and girls how to become a Christian. Tell kids how they can respond, and provide counselors to speak with each kid individually. Guide counselors to use open-ended questions to allow kids to determine the direction of the conversation.

Encourage boys and girls to ask their parents, small group leaders, or other adults any questions they may have about becoming a Christian.

Key passage (5 minutes)

• Key Passage Slide or Poster
• "I'm Not Ashamed" song

Invite any kids who have memorized the key passage to recite it from memory. Then display the key passage poster. Ask all the girls to read it aloud, and then ask the boys.

Leader • Who wrote this verse? (*Paul*)

What was Paul not ashamed of? (*the gospel*)

The gospel is God's power for what? (*salvation*)

Who can be saved? (*everyone who believes*)

Allow a couple of volunteers to lead the group in singing "I'm Not Ashamed."

Discussion starter video (4 minutes)

• "Unit 35 Session 4" discussion starter video

Tip: Affirm kids' questions, but do not feel like you need to provide answers.

Leader • When Paul was in Athens, he talked to some people who worshiped a god they did not know. These people liked to think deep thoughts about life. Do you have any deep questions?

Show the "Unit 35 Session 4" video. Invite kids to share any big questions they have about God.

Leader • Those are some good questions. Paul probably spent a lot of time answering the people's questions. But you don't have to be an expert thinker to understand the good news about Jesus.

Sing (4 minutes)

• "Shake" song

Leader • Before we trust in Jesus as Savior, we are a lot like the people in Athens. We might not worship idols made out of silver or stone, but we might worship other things or even ourselves.

God changes our hearts when we trust in Jesus as Lord and Savior. Only the Lord deserves our worship. Let's sing and celebrate the way Jesus changes us.

Play the song "Shake" and encourage kids to sing along.

Prayer (2 minutes)

Leader • *Who deserves our worship? Only the Lord—the one true God—deserves our worship.* Before you go to small groups, let's pray.

Lead kids in a time of prayer. Pray for people who do not know Jesus as Lord and Savior. Ask God for opportunities to tell others the good news about Jesus. Praise Him for sending Jesus to save us from our sins and change our hearts so we want to worship Him.

Dismiss to small groups

The Gospel: God's Plan for Me

Ask kids if they have ever heard the word *gospel*. Clarify that the word *gospel* means "good news." It is the message about Christ, the kingdom of God, and salvation. Use the following guide to share the gospel with kids.

God rules. Explain to kids that the Bible tells us God created everything, and He is in charge of everything. Invite a volunteer to read Genesis 1:1 from the Bible. Read Revelation 4:11 or Colossians 1:16-17 aloud and explain what these verses mean.

We sinned. Tell kids that since the time of Adam and Eve, everyone has chosen to disobey God. (Romans 3:23) The Bible calls this sin. Because God is holy, God cannot be around sin. Sin separates us from God and deserves God's punishment of death. (Romans 6:23)

God provided. Choose a child to read John 3:16 aloud. Say that God sent His Son, Jesus, the perfect solution to our sin problem, to rescue us from the punishment we deserve. It's something we, as sinners, could never earn on our own. Jesus alone saves us. Read and explain Ephesians 2:8-9.

Jesus gives. Share with kids that Jesus lived a perfect life, died on the cross for our sins, and rose again. Because Jesus gave up His life for us, we can be welcomed into God's family for eternity. This is the best gift ever! Read Romans 5:8; 2 Corinthians 5:21; or 1 Peter 3:18.

We respond. Tell kids that they can respond to Jesus. Read Romans 10:9-10,13. Review these aspects of our response: Believe in your heart that Jesus alone saves you through what He's already done on the cross. Repent, turning from self and sin to Jesus. Tell God and others that your faith is in Jesus.

Offer to talk with any child who is interested in responding to Jesus.

Small Group LEADER

Session Title: Paul Preached in Europe
Bible Passage: Acts 17:1–18:21
Big Picture Question: Who deserves our worship? Only the Lord—the one true God—deserves our worship.
Key Passage: Romans 1:16
Unit Christ Connection: God chose Paul to be a witness to all he had seen and heard of the risen Christ.

Key passage activity (5 minutes)

- Key Passage Poster
- dry erase board
- dry erase markers

Write the key passage on a dry erase board so all of the kids can read it. Intentionally write several incorrect words or phrases. (Example: *I am not ashamed of the <u>Bible</u>, because it is <u>my</u> power for <u>success</u> to everyone who <u>doubts</u>, first to the <u>boys</u>, and also to the <u>girls</u>.*)

Challenge kids to recognize the errors and correct the verse. Then show the key passage poster and guide kids to read it aloud together. If time allows, rewrite the verse and play again.

Say • Who wrote these words? (*Paul*)

• This verse tells us that people are saved by believing in Jesus. Paul shared the gospel with the Jews and with the non-Jews. He knew the gospel is good news for everyone to hear.

Bible story review & Bible skills (10 minutes)

- Bibles, 1 per kid
- Small Group Visual Pack
- large group of paper
- markers

Form two teams. Draw on a large sheet of paper a tic-tac-toe grid. Challenge kids to a game of tic-tac-toe. Explain that you will ask the first team a review question. If the team answers correctly, the team may mark an *X* on the tic-tac-toe board. If incorrect, play passes to the other team.

The first team to mark three *X*s or *O*s in a row wins.

Sample review questions:

Option: Retell or review the Bible story using the bolded text of the Bible story script.

1. With whom did Paul travel when he was in Europe? (*Silas, Acts 17:4*)

2. What city did Paul and Silas first travel to? (*Thessalonica, Acts 17:1*)

3. Who did Paul say was the Messiah? (*Jesus, Acts 17:3*)

4. What did the Bereans do when Paul preached? (*They studied the Scriptures to make sure he was telling the truth, Acts 17:11*)

5. What was the city of Athens full of? (*idols, Acts 17:16*)

6. Paul found an altar in Athens to which god? (*to an unknown god, Acts 17:23*)

7. Who did Paul meet in Corinth? (*Aquila and Priscilla, Acts 18:2*)

8. ***Who deserves our worship? Only the Lord—the one true God—deserves our worship.***

Say • The men of Athens worshiped a false god whom they did not know. Paul explained to the men God's plan of salvation. He said that only God should be worshiped. Paul talked about Jesus and the resurrection. People can know God because Jesus took the punishment for sin that separates people from God.

If you choose to review with boys and girls how to become a Christian, explain that kids are welcome to speak with you or another teacher if they have questions.

- **God rules.** God created and is in charge of everything. (Gen. 1:1; Rev. 4:11; Col. 1:16-17)
- **We sinned.** Since Adam and Eve, everyone has chosen to disobey God. (Rom. 3:23; 6:23)
- **God provided.** God sent His Son, Jesus, to rescue

us from the punishment we deserve. (John 3:16; Eph. 2:8-9)

- **Jesus gives.** Jesus lived a perfect life, died on the cross for our sins, and rose again so we can be welcomed into God's family. (Rom. 5:8; 2 Cor. 5:21; 1 Pet. 3:18)

- **We respond.** Believe that Jesus alone saves you. Repent. Tell God that your faith is in Jesus. (Rom. 10:9-10,13)

Activity choice (10 minutes)

Option 1: Create a creation

Invite kids to create with clay or play dough. Ask them to share what they are creating. Point out that as they shape the clay, they are the creators and the figures are their creation.

• clay or play dough

Say • The people in Athens did not worship the Lord. They worshiped many idols, things that were created by human hands. Paul taught about the one true God.

- Are the figures you created alive? (*no*)
- Do the figures you created have any power? (*no*)
- Do the figures you created deserve our worship? (*no*)
- ***Who deserves our worship? Only the Lord—the one true God—deserves our worship.***

Option 2: Maze game

• paper
• markers
• painter's tape

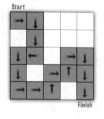

Prior to small group, use tape to mark a 5-by-5 grid on the floor. Write *Start* on one piece of paper and *Finish* on another. Label the designated squares.

Invite kids to play a maze game. Explain that there is a hidden path (see margin) from the start to finish. Number the kids, starting with 1. Allow the first player to begin. She will stand at the start space and move forward, sideways, or diagonally one space. If she moves to the correct space, say "yes," and allow her to continue. If not, say "no," and prompt the next player to try from the beginning.

Kids may work together to recall which spaces are part of the hidden path. Challenge kids to play silently, using only hand motions to communicate. When kids discover the secret path, every player should follow it to the finish space.

Say • Paul traveled many miles to visit people in different cities across Europe and Asia. He boldly shared the gospel, and he told the people in Athens to stop worshiping idols. Idols are made by people! They have no power and are not worthy of our worship.

• *Who deserves our worship? Only the Lord—the one true God—deserves our worship.*

Journal and prayer (5 minutes)

• pencils
• journals
• Bibles
• Journal Page, 1 per kid (enhanced CD)
• "Journey to Europe" activity page, 1 per kid

Distribute pencils and journal pages. Suggest kids write the big picture answer or draw a picture of a way they can worship God. Remind kids that people can worship God in many ways: by telling what God has done for them, giving offerings, praying, singing songs, or playing instruments.

Say • Paul taught that God made everything, and He is bigger than man-made idols. No one created God; He has always existed. Only God deserves our worship.

Invite kids to share prayer requests. Close the group in prayer, asking God to help us turn away from anything we might love instead of Him.

As time allows, lead kids to complete the activity page "Journey to Europe." You may choose to review the answers together. (*Across: 3. Athens; 5. synagogue; 6. Silas; 7. Corinth; Down: 1. Sabbath; 2. the Lord; 4. Messiah*)

Leader BIBLE STUDY

Paul traveled from place to place, teaching about Jesus and encouraging the believers. Luke, the writer of Acts, records that a major disturbance arose in Ephesus concerning the Way of the Lord. Ephesus was a large city in Asia Minor. It was a central location for politics, religions, and business.

Some men there made their living by making silver shrines for false gods, like the goddess Artemis. If people started to believe what Paul was saying, they could lose their livelihood! The men started a riot. Paul wanted to speak to the people, but the disciples would not let him. They feared for Paul's life. After the uproar was over, Paul left for Macedonia.

In Troas, a city in Macedonia, Paul spoke about Jesus late into the night. One young man named Eutychus (YOO tih kuhs) was sitting on a window sill, listening, when he fell asleep. He fell out the window from the third story and died. But Paul—through the power of God—brought him back to life.

Sometime later, Paul decided to go back to Jerusalem. Along the way, a prophet named Agabus came to Paul. He took Paul's belt and tied his own feet and hands. Then he said that the Jews in Jerusalem would bind Paul's hands and feet in the same way. Paul's friends begged him not to go. But Paul was not afraid to be arrested—or even to die—for the name of Jesus, so Paul kept going toward Jerusalem.

Paul told about Jesus even when he was in danger. Paul shared the gospel with people who didn't know Jesus. He told people to turn from their sins and trust in Jesus, and he encouraged believers in the church to keep loving Jesus. God changed the people's hearts, and they turned away from their sin. The good news about Jesus is powerful and life-giving.

Older Kids BIBLE STUDY OVERVIEW

Session Title: Paul's Third Journey
Bible Passage: Acts 18:18–21:16
Big Picture Question: What did Paul tell people to do? Paul told people to turn from their sins and trust in Jesus.
Key Passage: Romans 1:16
Unit Christ Connection: God chose Paul to be a witness to all he had seen and heard of the risen Christ.

Additional suggestions for specific groups are available at *gospelproject.com/kids/additional-resources*.

For free online training on how to lead a group, visit *ministrygrid.com/web/thegospelproject*.

The BIBLE STORY

Paul's Third Journey
Acts 18:18–21:16

Paul traveled with his friends Aquila and Priscilla from Corinth to Ephesus (EF uh suhs). Aquila and Priscilla stayed in Ephesus while **Paul visited churches throughout Asia. Paul helped the believers in the cities grow stronger in their faith.**

Paul made his way back to Ephesus. He went into the synagogue and spoke boldly for three months. He **tried to persuade the Jews to believe the truth about Jesus and the kingdom of God. But some of them refused to believe,** and they made fun of the Way. **Paul left the Jews** and went with other Christ-followers to a school. He talked with people there every day for two years. **Because of Paul's work, everyone in Asia—both Jews and Greeks—heard the truth about God.**

Trouble started in Ephesus. A man named Demetrius (dih MEE trih uhs) **made a living by making little silver shrines** of the goddess Artemis. **When Paul came around preaching about the one true God, Demetrius and the other silversmiths worried that people would stop worshiping gods made by hand. This would be bad for their business! So these men started shouting.** "Great is Artemis, the goddess of Ephesus!" they said. For two hours, they all said the same thing: "Great is Artemis of Ephesus! Great is Artemis of Ephesus!"

Paul waited for the trouble to stop, and then he left Ephesus. Paul and the men traveling with him went to the city of Troas (TROH az). **They met together to eat the Lord's Supper. Paul talked to the group until midnight. As he spoke, a young man named Eutychus** (YOO tih kuhs) **was sitting in the window. He listened to Paul talking and became very sleepy. When he fell asleep, he fell out the window—three stories down to the ground. Eutychus was dead, but Paul went to his side and put his arms around him, and Eutychus came back to life.** Paul told the other believers not to worry. **"He is alive now," Paul said. The believers took Eutychus home alive,** and they were greatly comforted.

Paul left Troas and traveled back toward Ephesus. He decided not to stop in Ephesus, but he asked the leaders of the church there to

meet him in a nearby city. **Paul said** to them, "I am obeying the Spirit and going to Jerusalem. I do not know what will happen to me there, but I know that trouble and jail wait for me. **I do not care about my own life. The most important thing is that I finish the work Jesus gave me to do.** I want to tell people the good news of God's grace." Paul and the church leaders prayed together, and they cried because they knew they might never see Paul again.

Paul sailed toward Jerusalem. Along the way, believers in Syria told him not to go. But Paul kept going. **When he was almost to Jerusalem, a prophet named Agabus** (AG uh buhs) **came to Paul. He took Paul's belt and tied it around his hands and feet. "The Holy Spirit tells me that the man who wears this belt will be tied up, just like this."** The believers begged Paul not to go to Jerusalem, but Paul could not be stopped. **"I am ready to go to jail—or even to die!—for the name of the Lord Jesus,"** Paul said.

Christ Connection: Paul shared the gospel with people who didn't know Jesus, and he encouraged believers in the church to keep loving Jesus. As people heard the message of salvation, God changed their hearts and they turned away from their sin. The good news about Jesus is powerful and life-giving.

Want to discover God's Word? Get *Bible Express*!
Invite kids to check out today's devotional to discover why Paul was willing to even die to spread the good news about Jesus. People turn away from sin and trust in Jesus as their Savior only after hearing the good news. (Romans 10:10) Since we have the gospel, we can't help but tell it to the whole world! Order in bulk, subscribe quarterly, or purchase individually. For more information, check out *www.lifeway.com/devotionals*.

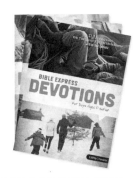

Small Group OPENING

Session Title: Paul's Third Journey
Bible Passage: Acts 18:18–21:16
Big Picture Question: What did Paul tell people to do? Paul told people to turn from their sins and trust in Jesus.
Key Passage: Romans 1:16
Unit Christ Connection: God chose Paul to be a witness to all he had seen and heard of the risen Christ.

Welcome time

Greet each kid as he or she arrives. Use this time to collect the offering, fill out attendance sheets, and help new kids connect to your group.

Activity page (5 minutes)

• "A Dangerous Journey" activity page, 1 per kid
• pencils

Distribute the activity page "A Dangerous Journey." Challenge kids to find the hidden words in the jungle scene: *gospel*, *Jesus*, *powerful*, and *life-giving*.

Say • Paul went on a journey to tell people about Jesus. When people heard the gospel—the good news about Jesus—many of them believed. The gospel is powerful. It gives life to people because when they trust in Jesus, God forgives their sin and they will live with Him forever.

Session starter (10 minutes)

Option 1: I'm going on a journey …
Invite boys and girls to sit in a circle. Establish a secret rule that players may only bring an item that has two syllables. Do not reveal the rule to players. Begin by saying the phrase, "I'm going on a journey, and I'm bringing a … "

then say an item that has two syllables. (Example: blan-ket.)

To figure out the rule, players should ask if they can bring items on the journey. They might say, "Can I bring a video game?" and you will say yes or no based on the secret rule. Continue around the circle as time allows.

Say • We are going to hear a Bible story today about Paul's third journey. Paul sure traveled a lot! Because of Paul's work, many people heard the truth about God.

Option 2: A long, long walk

• masking tape or painter's tape
• yardstick
• stopwatch
• calculator
• paper
• pencil

Mark a start line on the floor at one side of the room. Use a yardstick to measure 10 feet, and mark a finish line.

Choose a volunteer to walk from the start line to the finish line. Time how long it takes her to walk 10 feet.

Ask them how long they think it would take the volunteer to walk a mile? There are 5,280 feet in a mile; she would have to walk between the lines 528 times!

Calculate the approximate time it would take the volunteer to walk a mile. Use a calculator to multiply her time in seconds by 528. If she took 3 seconds to walk 10 feet, she could walk a mile in 1,584 seconds (26 minutes, 24 seconds).

Time other kids' walks and help them calculate how long they would take to walk a mile. Encourage them to walk casually to measure an accurate time. This is not a race!

Option: Calculate how long it would take to walk 2,500 miles. (*3,960,000 seconds or 45 days and 20 hours*)

Say • Today's Bible story is about Paul's third journey. On his journey, Paul traveled over 2,500 miles—about the width of the United States. Paul walked and sailed, and he also stopped and stayed in cities for a while. His journey lasted four years.

Transition to large group

Paul's Conversion and Ministry

Large Group LEADER

Session Title: Paul's Third Journey
Bible Passage: Acts 18:18–21:16
Big Picture Question: What did Paul tell people to do? Paul told people to turn from their sins and trust in Jesus.
Key Passage: Romans 1:16
Unit Christ Connection: God chose Paul to be a witness to all he had seen and heard of the risen Christ.

Countdown

• countdown video

Show the countdown video as your kids arrive, and set it to end as large group time begins.

Introduce the session (3 minutes)

• leader attire
• sunglasses
• camera

[Large Group Leader enters wearing sunglasses and a camera. Leader snaps a few pictures before greeting kids.]

Leader •Hi, everyone! [*Hold up camera and snap a picture.*] Looking good! I sure am glad to see you today. We are full speed ahead on our road trip. This trip has been going so fast, I'm making sure to take photos so I can remember everything that happened and all the places I've visited. Does anyone remember what we learned last week about Paul's time in Europe? [*Allow kids to share what they remember about the Bible story.*]

Paul went to Athens, where the people worshiped idols. Paul taught that *only the Lord—the one true God— deserves our worship.*

Timeline map (1 minute)

• Timeline Map

Leader •Let's see. Which of these pictures is for today's Bible story? Ah, here it is! Hey, this kind of looks like

Paul, but what happened to his beard and hair? The Bible says Paul shaved his head because of a promise he made to God. I'm sure his hair will grow back.

Anyway, Paul looks like he's on a ship. That makes a lot of sense because in today's Bible story, Paul spent four years traveling, and he traveled a long way. Sometimes he walked, but he traveled by ship a lot too.

Big picture question (1 minute)

Leader • Paul wasn't on a cruise. He traveled to so many different places because he obeyed God's call. God had a job for Paul. Paul went to each city and gave the people a message. *What did Paul tell people to do?* That's our big picture question today. Let's find out the answer.

Tell the Bible story (10 minutes)

• "Paul's Third Journey" video
• Bibles, 1 per kid
• Bible Story Picture Slide or Poster
• Big Picture Question Slide or Poster
• "Paul's Third Journey Map" (enhanced CD)

Open your Bible to Acts 18 and tell the Bible story in your own words, or show the Bible story video "Paul's Third Journey." As you review the Bible story, show the map of Paul's third journey and point out key locations: Corinth, Ephesus, Troas, and Jerusalem.

Leader • During Paul's third journey, three major things happened. First, he went to Ephesus. Paul went to the synagogue and talked to the people about Jesus. He was bold! *Paul told people to turn from their sins and trust in Jesus.* That's the answer to our big picture question. *What did Paul tell people to do? Paul told people to turn from their sins and trust in Jesus.*

Some of the men in Ephesus who made idols out of silver and gold wanted Paul to be quiet. If he turned the people to God, their business would be ruined! They made a living by selling little statues for people to worship. They made trouble for Paul, and he left.

Next, Paul and his friends went to Troas. They met together to eat the Lord's Supper. When a young man named Eutychus fell asleep and fell out the window to his death, God used Paul to bring him back to life!

Finally, Paul started heading back to Jerusalem. Paul was obedient to God's calling. He wanted to do the job God wanted him to do, even if it meant going to jail or dying. A prophet came and told Paul that he would be tied up in Jerusalem, but not even that would stop Paul. Paul's friends were sad, but they agreed that it was best for Paul to do what God wanted.

God blessed Paul's work. The Bible says that because of Paul's work, everyone in Asia heard the truth about God. [*See Acts 19:10.*] God changed people's hearts, and many people who heard the gospel believed and were saved. Paul also encouraged believers to keep following God and living lives that honored Him.

The Gospel: God's Plan for Me (optional)

Using Scripture and the guide provided, explain to boys and girls how to become a Christian. Tell kids how they can respond, and provide counselors to speak with each kid individually. Guide counselors to use open-ended questions to allow kids to determine the direction of the conversation.

Encourage boys and girls to ask their parents, small group leaders, or other adults any questions they may have about becoming a Christian.

Key passage (5 minutes)

• Key Passage Slide or Poster
• "I'm Not Ashamed" song

Show the key passage poster and choose a volunteer to read it aloud. If any kids can recite Romans 1:16 from memory, hide the poster and challenge them to do so.

Leader •Paul wrote this verse in his letter to the church in

Rome. He said that the gospel went first to the Jews and then to the Greeks, or non-Jews.

When we look at the Old Testament, God worked through the Jewish people to get people ready for Jesus' coming into the world. When Paul preached, he went to the synagogues first, where the Jews worshiped. Some of them believed, but some of them did not. So Paul went to tell the non-Jews about Jesus too. Paul knew that the gospel is for everyone. Let's sing.

Invite kids to join you in singing "I'm Not Ashamed."

Discussion starter video (5 minutes)

• "Unit 35 Session 5" discussion starter video

Leader • When Paul's friends heard that he might be arrested or killed in Jerusalem, what did they tell him? They told him not to go! Paul faced a difficult situation, but did he give up? No. Watch this.

Show the "Unit 35 Session 5" video. Then lead kids to talk about times they have struggled to do something, such as learn an instrument or play a sport. Emphasize that Paul said the most important thing was not that he lived a safe and easy life but that people heard about Jesus!

Sing (3 minutes)

• "Shake" song

Leader • Paul was serious about the gospel! Can anyone tell me what Paul was like before he met Jesus? Yes, Paul hated the church and tried to stop people from telling others about Jesus. Now he risked everything—his freedom and even his life—to share the good news about Jesus with the whole world.

Paul was changed because that's what the gospel does. It changes us! Sing with me.

Lead kids to sign the song "Shake" together.

Prayer (2 minutes)

Leader • I've had such a great time with you learning all about Paul's journeys. Will you come back next time? We have one more journey to learn about and it might be the most adventurous of them all! Before you go, let's pray.

Lord, we come to You as sinners. We need Your mercy. Lead us to turn away from our sins and trust in Jesus. Thank You for sending Jesus to take away our sins so we can be with You forever. We love You. Amen.

Dismiss to small groups

The Gospel: God's Plan for Me

Ask kids if they have ever heard the word *gospel*. Clarify that the word *gospel* means "good news." It is the message about Christ, the kingdom of God, and salvation. Use the following guide to share the gospel with kids.

God rules. Explain to kids that the Bible tells us God created everything, and He is in charge of everything. Invite a volunteer to read Genesis 1:1 from the Bible. Read Revelation 4:11 or Colossians 1:16-17 aloud and explain what these verses mean.

We sinned. Tell kids that since the time of Adam and Eve, everyone has chosen to disobey God. (Romans 3:23) The Bible calls this sin. Because God is holy, God cannot be around sin. Sin separates us from God and deserves God's punishment of death. (Romans 6:23)

God provided. Choose a child to read John 3:16 aloud. Say that God sent His Son, Jesus, the perfect solution to our sin problem, to rescue us from the punishment we deserve. It's something we, as sinners, could never earn on our own. Jesus alone saves us. Read and explain Ephesians 2:8-9.

Jesus gives. Share with kids that Jesus lived a perfect life, died on the cross for our sins, and rose again. Because Jesus gave up His life for us, we can be welcomed into God's family for eternity. This is the best gift ever! Read Romans 5:8; 2 Corinthians 5:21; or 1 Peter 3:18.

We respond. Tell kids that they can respond to Jesus. Read Romans 10:9-10,13. Review these aspects of our response: Believe in your heart that Jesus alone saves you through what He's already done on the cross. Repent, turning from self and sin to Jesus. Tell God and others that your faith is in Jesus.

Offer to talk with any child who is interested in responding to Jesus.

Small Group LEADER

Session Title: Paul's Third Journey
Bible Passage: Acts 18:18–21:16
Big Picture Question: What did Paul tell people to do? Paul told people to turn from their sins and trust in Jesus.
Key Passage: Romans 1:16
Unit Christ Connection: God chose Paul to be a witness to all he had seen and heard of the risen Christ.

Key passage activity (5 minutes)

• Key Passage Poster

Count off kids by twos. Instruct all the *ones* to stand on the right side of the room and all the *twos* to stand on the left side. Ask a volunteer to demonstrate what an echo sounds like. She should shout a word and then repeat it, more quietly with each repetition.

Explain that you will say a few words of the key passage. The kids on the left side of the room should repeat it after you, speaking loudly. Then the kids at the right side of the room will say it quietly.

Break the key passage into two- or three-syllable phrases. Allow kids to echo the verse after you. Then allow kids to switch groups so the loud group will speak quietly, and the quiet group will be loud.

Bible story review & Bible skills (10 minutes)

• Bibles, 1 per kid
• Small Group Visual Pack
• index cards
• marker

Write the following review questions and answers on separate index cards. Make enough for each kid to have one card. Distribute the cards. Instruct kids with question cards to stand. They should walk up to someone with an answer card (someone who is sitting) and ask the question. The sitting player should read her answer.

Option: Retell or review the Bible story using the bolded text of the Bible story script.

If the answer matches the question, the pair should stand together at the front of the room. If not, the standing player should move on to ask another sitting player. Play until kids all find their partners. If time remains, lead each pair to read their question and answer to the group.

1. What city did Paul visit first on his third journey? (*Ephesus, Acts 18:18-19*)

2. How many months did Paul speak at the synagogue? (*three months, Acts 19:8*)

3. How did the Jews respond to Paul's message? (*Some Jews refused to believe, Acts 19:9*)

4. What did the businessmen in Ephesus shout? (*"Great is Artemis of Ephesus!" Acts 19:28,34*)

5. Where did Paul go when he left Ephesus? (*Troas, Acts 20:6*)

6. What happened to the young man listening to Paul? (*He fell asleep and fell out the window, Acts 20:9*)

7. Where did Paul tell the church leaders he was going? (*Jerusalem, Acts 20:22*)

8. What did Paul say is the most important thing? (*to finish the work that Jesus gave him to do, Acts 20:24*)

9. What did the prophet say would happen to Paul? (*He would be tied up, Acts 21:10*)

10. **What did Paul tell people to do? Paul told people to turn from their sins and trust in Jesus.**

Say • Paul shared the gospel with people who didn't know Jesus, and he encouraged believers in the church to keep loving Jesus. God changed the people's hearts, and they turned away from their sin. The good news about Jesus is powerful and life-giving.

If you choose to review with boys and girls how to become a Christian, explain that kids are welcome to speak with you or another teacher if they have questions.

- **God rules.** God created and is in charge of everything. (Gen. 1:1; Rev. 4:11; Col. 1:16-17)
- **We sinned.** Since Adam and Eve, everyone has chosen to disobey God. (Rom. 3:23; 6:23)
- **God provided.** God sent His Son, Jesus, to rescue us from the punishment we deserve. (John 3:16; Eph. 2:8-9)
- **Jesus gives.** Jesus lived a perfect life, died on the cross for our sins, and rose again so we can be welcomed into God's family. (Rom. 5:8; 2 Cor. 5:21; 1 Pet. 3:18)
- **We respond.** Believe that Jesus alone saves you. Repent. Tell God that your faith is in Jesus. (Rom. 10:9-10,13)

Activity choice (10 minutes)

• small ball or beanbag

Option 1: Turn and trust

Show kids the small ball or beanbag. Share the code words, "turn and trust," and prompt kids to repeat them back to you. Give kids a chance to move around the room with their hands clasped behind their backs, observing but not touching. Then instruct kids to sit in their seats with their heads down and eyes covered.

Hide the small ball in plain sight. Tell the kids how to play the game: First, open your eyes and walk around the room with your hands behind your back. When you see the object, return to your seat and say, "Turn and trust."

Encourage kids to continue searching for a few seconds after they find the object so they don't reveal the ball's location. Continue playing until everyone finds the ball.

Say • *What did Paul tell people to do? Paul told people to turn from their sins and trust in Jesus.*

Option 2: Candy color sort

- large bowl
- plastic spoons, 1 per kid
- small cups
- permanent marker
- candy-coated chocolate pieces
- Allergy Alert (enhanced CD)

Fill a large bowl with candy-coated chocolate pieces. Label small cups with the colors of the chocolate pieces (*blue*, *green*, *orange*, *yellow*, *red*, *brown*).

Form three to six groups. Guide groups to stand single file at one end of the room. Position the bowl at the center of the room and line the cups on the other end of the room.

Assign each group a color and give each kid a spoon. When you say go, the first player in each line will run to the bowl, scoop up one piece of candy in his team's color, and drop it into the correct cup. Then the player should go to the end of his group's line. The next player will do the same.

Allow kids to play for a few minutes, and then call time. Count the pieces in each team's cup to see which team collected the most candies. Guide the winning team to ask the big picture question. The other teams should take turns giving the answer.

Say • *What did Paul tell people to do? Paul told people to turn from their sins and trust in Jesus.*

Journal and prayer (5 minutes)

- pencils
- journals
- Bibles
- Journal Page, 1 per kid (enhanced CD)
- "Trace Paul's Path" activity page, 1 per kid

Distribute journal pages and suggest kids write letters to Paul, imagining what they would tell him as he got ready to go to Jerusalem, where he knew he could be arrested or murdered for telling people about Jesus.

Invite kids to share prayer requests. Pray for missionaries around the world who risk everything to spread the gospel.

As time allows, lead kids to complete the activity page "Trace Paul's Path." Boys and girls should unscramble the names of the cities to figure out where Paul traveled between Antioch in Syria and Jerusalem. (*1. Antioch; 2. Ephesus; 3. Macedonia; 4. Greece; 5. Troas; 6. Miletus; 7. Tyre; 8. Jerusalem*)

Leader BIBLE STUDY

Through the prophet Agabus, the Holy Spirit had told Paul that he would be bound if he went back to Jerusalem, and that's exactly what happened. Some Jews there accused him of teaching against God. They tried to kill him, but a Roman army commander stopped them and arrested Paul. Paul had been born a Roman citizen, and his status as such protected him from an unjustified beating.

While in prison, the Lord told Paul that he would one day teach about Him in Rome. Rome was one of the most powerful and influential cities of that day. But Paul spent two years in prison before he was sent to Rome to be heard by Caesar.

Along the way, the ship Paul was sailing on wrecked near the island of Malta. But God kept everyone safe, and Paul had a chance to pray for people who lived on the island. He even healed some of them.

Months later, Paul reached Rome. He was still a prisoner, but he was allowed to stay in a house by himself with a guard. He taught everyone who visited him about Jesus and the kingdom of God. Nothing—not beatings or shipwrecks or prisons—could keep Paul from preaching about Jesus.

Paul went to jail for teaching about Jesus, but God made the way for Paul to continue spreading the good news of Jesus in Rome. Everyone there knew Paul was in prison for teaching about the Messiah. (Phil. 1:12-13) God protected Paul so he could keep telling people about Jesus. No punishment or suffering stopped Paul from telling others about Jesus.

As you teach, prompt kids to think about whether or not anything could stop them from telling others about Jesus. Pray that God would give them boldness and that He would grow them up to live on mission for Christ. Remind kids that the Holy Spirit gives believers power to share the gospel all over the world so people will know and love Jesus.

Older Kids BIBLE STUDY OVERVIEW

Session Title: Paul's Ministry to Rome
Bible Passage: Acts 21:17–28:31
Big Picture Question: How did God help Paul on his journey? God protected Paul so he could keep telling people about Jesus.
Key Passage: Romans 1:16
Unit Christ Connection: God chose Paul to be a witness to all he had seen and heard of the risen Christ.

U N I T
35

6

Additional suggestions for specific groups are available at *gospelproject.com/kids/additional-resources*.

For free online training on how to lead a group, visit *ministrygrid.com/web/thegospelproject*.

The BIBLE STORY

Paul's Ministry to Rome
Acts 21:17–28:31

Paul was in Jerusalem, and the believers there were happy to see him.
One day, Paul went to the temple. Some Jews saw him there, and they
gathered a crowd against him. The crowd **grabbed Paul and dragged him
out of the temple.**

**As the crowd was trying to kill Paul, the commander of the Roman
army stopped them.** He arrested Paul. **"What has this man done
wrong?" the commander asked. But too many people in the crowd
were shouting,** and the commander could not figure out what Paul had
done wrong. The crowd shouted, **"Kill him!"**

**Paul was taken to the army barracks. He asked the commander if
he could speak to the crowd.** Paul told the people that he had been like
them; he used to arrest the believers and throw them into jail. But Jesus
changed Paul! **Paul explained how he became a believer and how Jesus
told him to take the good news to the Gentiles. This made the Jews
even angrier.** Now they really wanted Paul dead! **The army commander
took Paul inside the barracks.**

**The next night, the Lord came to Paul and said, "Have courage!
You told people about Me in Jerusalem. You must also tell people in
Rome."**

Paul soon heard that the Jewish leaders had a plan to kill him.
He told the army commander about the plan. **Since Paul was a Roman
citizen, the commander protected Paul and decided to send him to
Caesarea** (SESS uh REE uh), a city by the sea. **Paul was a prisoner in
Caesarea for two years. Then the governor sent him to Rome.**

Paul got on a ship with other prisoners going to Rome. An army
officer named Julius was in charge of guarding them. **But the sailing was
rough. A storm came, and everyone on the ship—276 people—was
afraid they would die. God sent an angel to Paul. The angel told Paul
to not be afraid. God would save the lives of everyone on the ship.**

**No one on the ship died in the storm, but the ship wrecked on an
island** called Malta. **Paul and all the others swam to shore.** The people

who lived on the island took care of them. **Paul met with people on the island who were sick. He prayed for them and healed them.**

Finally, Paul got on another ship and sailed to Rome. Paul was still a prisoner, but instead of going to jail, Paul was allowed to live by himself in a house. A soldier stayed with him to guard him. People came to Paul's house and listened to him speak. He taught people about the kingdom of God and about the Lord Jesus Christ, and some of the people believed.

Christ Connection: Paul's work to spread the good news of Jesus continued in Rome. No punishment or suffering kept Paul from telling others about Jesus. The Holy Spirit gives believers power to share the gospel all over the world so people will know and love Jesus.

Want to discover God's Word? Get *Bible Express*!

Invite kids to check out today's devotional to discover the power of the gospel and our role in the Great Commission. (Matthew 28:19) Even through beatings, shipwrecks, and imprisonment, Paul was not ashamed of the gospel of Jesus Christ. Order in bulk, subscribe quarterly, or purchase individually. For more information, check out *www.lifeway.com/devotionals*.

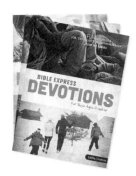

Small Group OPENING

Session Title: Paul's Ministry to Rome
Bible Passage: Acts 21:17–28:31
Big Picture Question: How did God help Paul on his journey? God protected Paul so he could keep telling people about Jesus.
Key Passage: Romans 1:16
Unit Christ Connection: God chose Paul to be a witness to all he had seen and heard of the risen Christ.

Welcome time

Greet each kid as he or she arrives. Use this time to collect the offering, fill out attendance sheets, and help new kids connect to your group. Invite kids to share one thing they would want with them if they were stuck on an island.

Activity page (5 minutes)

- "Totally Protected" activity page, 1 per kid
- pencils

Invite kids to complete the "Totally Protected" activity page. Give kids a couple of minutes to review each scene. Then call on volunteers to share what type of protective gear the athletes could use to keep them safe.

(*Possible answers: helmets, knee pads, mask, gloves, mitt, elbow pads, wrist pads, goggles*)

Say • Today's Bible story is about Paul and another of his journeys. On this journey, God kept Paul safe!

Session starter (10 minutes)

- masking tape or painter's tape

Option 1: Shipwreck!
Clear an area to play an active game. Mark a line on the floor in the middle of the room. The line should be long enough for all the kids to stand on it.

Instruct kids to line up and explain that you are the

captain, and they are the crew. You will give commands, the kids will perform specific actions or sounds. Before playing, teach kids the commands. Explain that you are all sailing on a dangerous sea, and everyone needs to work together and obey the captain's commands to survive.

- *Roll call*: Players must stand with their toes on the line, salute, and say, "Aye-aye, Captain!" The crew may not lower their salute until you say, "At ease."
- Crow's nest: Players act as if they're climbing a ladder to the crow's nest at the top of the main mast.
- *Swab the deck*: Players act like they're mopping.
- *Row to shore*: Players find a partner, simulate rowing, and sing "Row, Row, Row Your Boat."

To play, call out a command. Any kid who does not follow the command correctly or who is the last to obey should sit out. The goal is to be the last crew member standing.

Say • In today's Bible story, Paul found himself on a ship in some dangerous waters. Everyone on the ship was afraid they wouldn't survive. Do you think they did?

Option 2: Float a boat

- clay or play dough
- pennies
- tub of water
- paper towels (for cleanup)

Give each kid a golf ball-size lump of clay. Invite kids to use the clay to form a boat. Encourage creativity. If kids need help, suggest that they roll the clay into a ball and press in the center with their thumb. Then they could pinch the sides and flatten out the bottom.

Allow kids to test out their boats in a shallow tub of water. Provide pennies to see how much weight their boats can carry before they sink.

Say • In today's Bible story, Paul was in a boat that wrecked off an island. Are you ready to hear more?

Transition to large group

Paul's Conversion and Ministry

Large Group LEADER

Session Title: Paul's Ministry to Rome
Bible Passage: Acts 21:17–28:31
Big Picture Question: How did God help Paul on his journey? God
  protected Paul so he could keep telling people about Jesus.
Key Passage: Romans 1:16
Unit Christ Connection: God chose Paul to be a witness to all he had seen
  and heard of the risen Christ.

Countdown

• countdown video

Show the countdown video as your kids arrive, and set it to
end as large group time begins.

Introduce the session (2 minutes)

• leader attire
• postcards
• pencil

*[Large Group Leader enters carrying a pencil and a
stack of postcards. Leader jots a short note on a postcard,
reading it aloud.]*

Leader •Dear Mom, I just wanted to let you know that my
  road trip is going really well. I've seen so many things
  along the way. I will be home soon. Love, [*your name*].

  There! Hi, everyone! I'm just finishing up some
  postcards to mail back home. I like sending postcards to
  family and friends so they can see some of the places I
  visited on my travels. This is our last week on the road,
  and we're going to hear the last Bible story about Paul's
  journeys. Let's get started.

Timeline map (2 minutes)

• Timeline Map

Point to each Bible story picture on the timeline map as you
briefly review previous stories of Paul's journeys.

  Leader •After Paul believed in Jesus, he started traveling to many different cities, telling people the good news of the gospel. Paul was a missionary. *What is a missionary?* *A missionary is someone who obeys God's call to go and tell others the good news about Jesus.*

Next, Paul went on a second journey. This time he went with his friend Silas. They traveled to Macedonia and stopped in the city of Philippi. *What did Paul do as he traveled? Paul started churches in other cities and taught people about Jesus.*

Then Paul spent some time in Europe. The people worshiped many idols, but Paul taught them that *only the Lord—the one true God—deserves our worship.*

On his third journey, Paul went to Ephesus. Then he went to Troas before heading to Jerusalem. Paul shared the gospel with people who didn't know Jesus. *Paul told people to turn from their sins and trust in Jesus.*

Now here is the picture for today's Bible story. Oh my! Paul looks to be in a bit of trouble here. Those men do not look like Paul's friends.

Big picture question (1 minute)

Leader • Paul faced a lot of trouble and suffering as he traveled and told people about Jesus. Not everyone was happy to hear the good news about Jesus, but Paul was not alone. Our big picture question is, *How did God help Paul on his journey?* Listen closely to find the answer!

Tell the Bible story (10 minutes)

Open your Bible to Acts 21 and tell the Bible story in your own words, or show the Bible story video "Paul's Ministry to Rome." As you review the story, show the map of Paul's journey to Rome and point out the key locations: Jerusalem, Caesarea (SESS uh REE uh), the island of Malta, and Rome.

- "Paul's Ministry to Rome" video
- Bibles, 1 per kid
- Bible Story Picture Slide or Poster
- Big Picture Question Slide or Poster
- "Paul's Journey to Rome Map" (enhanced CD)

Leader •The things Paul was teaching—that Jesus is God's Son and that a person could be saved by trusting in Him—did not sit well with the Jews. They didn't agree with Paul's teachings, and they tried to kill him.

Fortunately, they did not kill Paul. A commander of the Roman army came along and rescued Paul. And by rescued, I mean he put Paul into prison.

While Paul was in prison, God told him that he was going to go to Rome to tell people about Jesus. Paul was in prison for a couple years before he finally got on a ship heading to Rome. The ship had many prisoners onboard, along with some soldiers who looked after them. When the ship wrecked near the island of Malta, no one on the ship was hurt. But the soldiers didn't want the prisoners to escape, so they thought about killing all the prisoners! Fortunately they decided not to.

By the time Paul finally got to Rome, he was still a prisoner. But instead of being in a prison cell, Paul was allowed to live in a house by himself. A soldier stayed there to guard Paul, but people were allowed to visit him. Paul taught the people who came to see him, and some of them believed in Jesus.

Paul came so close to being killed on his journey! *How did God help Paul on his journey? God protected Paul so he could keep telling people about Jesus.* God worked everything out so that people could hear the gospel and believe. God is still at work today, giving believers strength and courage through the Holy Spirit so that people all over the world will hear the gospel and believe.

The Gospel: God's Plan for Me (optional)

Using Scripture and the guide provided, explain to boys and girls how to become a Christian. Tell kids how they can respond, and provide counselors to speak with each kid individually. Guide counselors to use open-ended questions to allow kids to determine the direction of the conversation.

Encourage boys and girls to ask their parents, small group leaders, or other adults any questions they may have about becoming a Christian.

Key passage (5 minutes)

- Key Passage Slide or Poster
- "I'm Not Ashamed" song

Show the key passage poster. Lead kids to say the passage together. Give each kid a chance to recite Romans 1:16 from memory.

Leader • Can anyone tell me what this verse means? (*Paul wrote these words. He was not embarrassed of the good news about Jesus. Paul believed that the gospel is for everyone—Jews and non-Jews. By believing the gospel, people are saved. When people trust in Jesus, God forgives their sin and they will live with Him forever.*)

Play "I'm Not Ashamed" song and invite kids to sing along.

Discussion starter video (4 minutes)

- "Unit 35 Session 6" discussion starter video

Leader • Think about what Paul went through just because he obeyed God and told people about Jesus! What would you do? Watch this video.

Show the "Unit 35 Session 6" video.

Leader • Paul faced some scary situations when he told people about Jesus. People hated him, and some people even tried to kill him! He was beaten and thrown into jail. Is there anything that would stop you from telling people about Jesus?

Guide kids to share their thoughts. Point out that Jesus said that people would hate or hurt His followers. But He said to not be afraid. (See Matt. 10:16-20,26-28.)

Sing (4 minutes)

• "Shake" song

Leader • Wow. Paul's life sure changed. Remember when we first learned about Paul? He was going by the name *Saul*, and he did everything he could to stop the church! He arrested believers and even approved of them being killed! Everything changed when Paul met Jesus. Paul realized that Jesus is the Lord. He is God's Son. When we trust in Him, we are changed too! Let's sing.

Lead boys and girls to sing "Shake."

Prayer (2 minutes)

Leader • Nothing stopped Paul from telling people about Jesus! Before you go to your small groups, let's pray.

Lead kids in prayer. Thank God for protecting Paul and for working all things—including a shipwreck and imprisonment—together for Paul's good. Point out that *God protected Paul so he could keep telling people about Jesus.* Thank God for protecting us. Ask Him for courage and boldness to faithfully spread the gospel.

Dismiss to small groups

The Gospel: God's Plan for Me

Ask kids if they have ever heard the word *gospel*. Clarify that the word *gospel* means "good news." It is the message about Christ, the kingdom of God, and salvation. Use the following guide to share the gospel with kids.

God rules. Explain to kids that the Bible tells us God created everything, and He is in charge of everything. Invite a volunteer to read Genesis 1:1 from the Bible. Read Revelation 4:11 or Colossians 1:16-17 aloud and explain what these verses mean.

We sinned. Tell kids that since the time of Adam and Eve, everyone has chosen to disobey God. (Romans 3:23) The Bible calls this sin. Because God is holy, God cannot be around sin. Sin separates us from God and deserves God's punishment of death. (Romans 6:23)

God provided. Choose a child to read John 3:16 aloud. Say that God sent His Son, Jesus, the perfect solution to our sin problem, to rescue us from the punishment we deserve. It's something we, as sinners, could never earn on our own. Jesus alone saves us. Read and explain Ephesians 2:8-9.

Jesus gives. Share with kids that Jesus lived a perfect life, died on the cross for our sins, and rose again. Because Jesus gave up His life for us, we can be welcomed into God's family for eternity. This is the best gift ever! Read Romans 5:8; 2 Corinthians 5:21; or 1 Peter 3:18.

We respond. Tell kids that they can respond to Jesus. Read Romans 10:9-10,13. Review these aspects of our response: Believe in your heart that Jesus alone saves you through what He's already done on the cross. Repent, turning from self and sin to Jesus. Tell God and others that your faith is in Jesus.

Offer to talk with any child who is interested in responding to Jesus.

Small Group LEADER

Session Title: Paul's Ministry to Rome
Bible Passage: Acts 21:17–28:31
Big Picture Question: How did God help Paul on his journey? God protected Paul so he could keep telling people about Jesus.
Key Passage: Romans 1:16
Unit Christ Connection: God chose Paul to be a witness to all he had seen and heard of the risen Christ.

Key passage activity (5 minutes)

- Key Passage Poster
- index cards
- tape

Write each word of the key passage on a separate index card. Mix up the cards and tape them to a table or wall.

Invite kids to take turns slapping the cards in order as they say Romans 1:16. If kids need help, display the key passage poster and guide everyone to read it together.

Say • Paul was not ashamed of the gospel. The gospel is the good news that Jesus lived the perfect life we fail to live, and He died the death we deserve for our sin. When we trust in Jesus, God forgives our sin and we can live with Him forever.

Bible story review & Bible skills (10 minutes)

- Bibles, 1 per kid
- Small Group Visual Pack
- sticky notes
- marker

Consider retelling or reviewing the Bible story using the bolded text of the Bible story script.

Write the following references on separate sticky notes: *Acts 21:26-30*; *Acts 27:39-44*; and *Acts 28:16,30-31*. Form three groups, and give each group a sticky note. Provide Bibles for kids to look up and read their assigned passages.

Explain that group members should work together to plan out a skit for their assigned passage. Kids may act out the scene using classroom props. Encourage dialogue.

Groups may consider choosing a narrator to read the Bible passage aloud as other group members act. After each group performs, ask a couple of true-false questions to review:

Acts 21:26-30

1. The Jews were happy to see Paul and wanted to be his friend. (*false*)
2. The people rushed together, grabbed Paul, and dragged him out of the temple. (*true*)

Acts 27:39-44

1. The soldiers on the ship did not recognize the island. (*true*)
2. The soldiers killed all the prisoners so that they could not escape. (*false*)

Acts 28:16,30-31

1. Paul was thrown into a Roman prison with dozens of other prisoners. (*false*)
2. No one visited Paul, and he didn't talk to anyone for two years. (*false*)

Say • *How did God help Paul on his journey? God protected Paul so he could keep telling people about Jesus.*

• Paul's work to spread the good news of Jesus continued in Rome. No punishment or suffering stopped Paul from telling others about Jesus. The Holy Spirit gives believers power to share the gospel all over the world so people will know and love Jesus.

If you choose to review with boys and girls how to become a Christian, explain that kids are welcome to speak with you or another teacher if they have questions.

• **God rules.** God created and is in charge of everything. (Gen. 1:1; Rev. 4:11; Col. 1:16-17)
• **We sinned.** Since Adam and Eve, everyone has chosen to disobey God. (Rom. 3:23; 6:23)
• **God provided.** God sent His Son, Jesus, to rescue

us from the punishment we deserve. (John 3:16; Eph. 2:8-9)

- **Jesus gives.** Jesus lived a perfect life, died on the cross for our sins, and rose again so we can be welcomed into God's family. (Rom. 5:8; 2 Cor. 5:21; 1 Pet. 3:18)

- **We respond.** Believe that Jesus alone saves you. Repent. Tell God that your faith is in Jesus. (Rom. 10:9-10,13)

Activity choice (10 minutes)

- chairs or cones, 1 per kid

Option 1: I'll tell my neighbor

Arrange chairs or a cone in a circle, one chair per kid. Guide kids to sit in the chairs. Choose one kid to stand in the center of the circle to be the leader. Remove that kid's chair from the circle. Explain that the leader will begin the game by saying, "I'll tell my neighbor about Jesus, especially my neighbor who … "

The leader will complete the sentence with a basic description such as " … who has a brother," " … who was born in March," or " … whose favorite color is orange."

As soon as the leader is finished with the statement, everyone (including the leader) who the statement describes moves from his chair to an empty chair that is not right next to him. The player left without a chair becomes the leader in the center of the circle.

Say • Whom can you tell about Jesus? Paul spent the rest of his life telling people—Jews and non-Jews—about Jesus. The gospel is not just for a certain group of people. The gospel is for everyone.

- *How did God help Paul on his journey? God protected Paul so he could keep telling people about Jesus.*

Option 2: Paper chains

- strips of paper
- tape
- Bible

Provide 1-by-8½-inch strips of paper. Show kids how to tape together the ends of one strip to form a loop. Position a second strip of paper through the loop. Again, tape together the ends of the paper.

Guide kids to continue looping and taping paper to form a long chain. Kids may work in a group or they may work independently and then join all their chains together.

As kids work, remind kids that Paul spent a lot of time in prison because he told people about Jesus. But Paul was not upset about being a prisoner. In fact, God used Paul's imprisonment for good. Read Philippians 1:12-20. Explain that Paul wrote these words to a church in Philippi.

Say • Paul was glad to be in chains for Jesus' sake. Nothing stopped Paul from telling others about Jesus. More than anything else, Paul wanted Jesus to be honored with his life.

Journal and prayer (5 minutes)

- pencils
- journals
- Bibles
- Journal Page, 1 per kid (enhanced CD)
- "Go, Paul, Go!" activity page, 1 per kid

Distribute pencils and journal pages to the kids. Prompt kids to list friends they could invite to church next week. Encourage them to invite their friends and to tell their friends about Jesus. Invite kids to share prayer requests. Close the group in prayer, or allow a couple volunteers to close the group in prayer.

As time allows, lead kids to complete the activity page "Go, Paul, Go!" Kids should answer the questions to finish the statement. For example, the first answer is *no*, which corresponds to the letter *B*. Kids will write the word from box B (*stopped*) in the first blank space. When kids finish, they will discover the statement, *Nothing stopped Paul from telling others about Jesus.*

Unit 36: GOD'S PLAN FOR THE CHURCH IS FULFILLED

Big Picture Questions

Session 1:
What is the purpose of the church? The church exists to worship God, teach believers, and make disciples of Jesus.

Session 2:
When will Jesus return to earth? No one knows when Jesus will return except God Himself.

Session 3:
What did Jesus tell the churches about Himself? Jesus is the Alpha and the Omega—the beginning and the end.

Session 4:
What will we do after Jesus returns? God will live with His people, and we will enjoy Him forever.

Unit 36: GOD'S PLAN FOR THE CHURCH IS FULFILLED

Unit Description: The church is God's plan to bring praise and glory to Jesus. One day, Jesus will come back to earth. He will undo every bad thing caused by sin, and those who trust in Him will be with Him and enjoy Him forever.

Unit Key Passage:
Revelation 22:12-13

Unit Christ Connection:
Jesus is making all things new.

Session 1:
Church Responsibility
1 Corinthians 1–16

Session 2:
Christ's Return Is Anticipated
2 Thessalonians 1–3

Session 3:
God's Warning to Seven Churches
Revelation 1–3

Session 4:
Jesus Christ Will Return
Revelation 19–22

Leader BIBLE STUDY

In the first century, the city of Corinth was an important destination in the Roman Empire. Corinth was located on a narrow area of land that connected the southern end of the Greek peninsula with the mainland to the north. When Paul visited Corinth on his missionary journeys, the city was full of people with various cultural backgrounds. Many of them worshiped Greek gods. Temples and shrines to these gods were scattered throughout the city.

Corinth was a strategic place to plant a church. Paul arrived in Corinth and met Aquila and his wife, Priscilla. Paul stayed with them for a year and a half. On the Sabbath Day, Paul went to the synagogues to teach God's message to the people. When the Jews refused to believe that Jesus is the Messiah, Paul preached to the Gentiles. Many Corinthians believed and were baptized. (Acts 18:1-18) Finally, Paul returned to Antioch in Syria.

About six years passed. Paul was in Ephesus when he heard a report that the church in Corinth was struggling. The people in the church were arguing and suing each other. In some ways, they lived just like the people in Corinth who were not believers. So Paul wrote a letter—the Book of First Corinthians—to the Corinthian church, not only to instruct them on how to live but to answer questions they had about the faith.

As you teach kids from First Corinthians, focus on a few of Paul's main points. He said that the Christian life is like a race, and a great reward awaits in heaven. (1 Cor. 9:24-27) Paul explained that the Lord decides what spiritual gifts to give to believers, and not every believer has the same gift. (1 Cor. 12:4-11) Then he reminded them of what is most important: the gospel of Jesus Christ. (1 Cor. 15:1-11)

Emphasize that Paul gave practical instructions so that the believers would know how to live in light of their salvation—not as a way to earn God's favor. Paul spent a significant portion of his ministry meeting with believers and encouraging them to keep the faith. Jesus' mission for the church is for believers to come together to worship God and to share the gospel.

Older Kids BIBLE STUDY OVERVIEW

Session Title: Church Responsibility
Bible Passage: 1 Corinthians 1–16
Big Picture Question: What is the purpose of the church? The church exists to worship God, teach believers, and make disciples of Jesus.
Key Passage: Revelation 22:12-13
Unit Christ Connection: Jesus is making all things new.

Small Group Opening

Large Group Leader

Small Group Leader

Additional suggestions for specific groups are available at *gospelproject.com/kids/additional-resources*.

For free online training on how to lead a group, visit *ministrygrid.com/web/thegospelproject*.

The BIBLE STORY

Church Responsibility
1 Corinthians 1–16

Paul wrote a letter to the church at Corinth. Years before, Paul helped start the church in Corinth. Now the church faced problems. Paul wrote his letter to help the people in the church. **He told them many things about how to follow Jesus.** Believers should live in such a way that people see them and know they belong to Jesus.

Paul said that living a life for Jesus is like running a race. All of the runners race, but only one receives the prize. "You must run to win," **Paul said. A believer's prize** is not a crown that will get rusty or break. A believer's reward **is in heaven. It is a crown that will last forever.**

Paul heard that when the church got together for a meal, people were divided. They did not get along. So **Paul reminded them of Jesus' words at the last supper.** On the night Jesus was betrayed, He took the bread, gave thanks, broke it, and said, "This is My body which is for you. Do this in remembrance of Me." In the same way, after supper He also took the cup and said, "This cup is the new covenant established by My blood. Do this, as often as you drink it, in remembrance of Me."

Then Paul explained that the Holy Spirit gives believers different types of spiritual gifts—talents and abilities for doing God's work. Not everyone has the same gift, but all of these gifts come from the Holy Spirit. Some people are wise, some have knowledge, and some have faith. **Every gift comes from God, and He decides who receives each gift.**

Paul said that believers must do everything in love. He explained what love is like. "Love is patient and kind. It does not want what someone else has or think less of others. Love is not quick to get angry and is happy with what is right. Love doesn't stop hoping, and love doesn't give up. Love never ends."

Finally, Paul reminded the church of the most important thing—the gospel. This is the good news about Jesus, and by believing it, people are saved. "Don't stop believing this message," Paul said. **"Christ died for our sins like the Scriptures said He would. He was buried and raised to life on the third day. Then He appeared to many people."**

As Paul finished the letter, he wrote, "Be alert and stand strong in the faith. Do everything with love."

Christ Connection: Jesus' mission for the church is for believers to come together to worship God and to share the gospel.

Want to discover God's Word? Get *Bible Express*!

Invite kids to check out today's devotional to discover why Paul reminded the Christians in the church at Corinth about the gospel of Jesus Christ. Anyone who calls upon the name of the Lord will be saved! (Romans 10:13) When the Holy Spirit dwells within us, He helps us grow to be more like Jesus. Order in bulk, subscribe quarterly, or purchase individually. For more information, check out *www.lifeway.com/devotionals*.

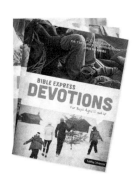

Small Group OPENING

Session Title: Church Responsibility
Bible Passage: 1 Corinthians 1–16
Big Picture Question: What is the purpose of the church? The church exists to worship God, teach believers, and make disciples of Jesus.
Key Passage: Revelation 22:12-13
Unit Christ Connection: Jesus is making all things new.

Welcome time

Greet each kid as he or she arrives. Use this time to collect the offering, fill out attendance sheets, and help new kids connect to your group. Invite kids to share things such as chores that they are responsible for doing at home.

Activity page (5 minutes)

- "Racetrack Rumble" activity page, 1 per kid
- game marker (coin, button, or so forth)
- Bibles, 1 per kid

Guide kids to find partners to play "Racetrack Rumble." Distribute the activity page and a game marker for each kid. Instruct each player to put his game marker at the start space. Each pair should designate a Player 1 and Player 2.

To play, both players will count to three and then hold out some fingers on one hand. Players will count how many fingers they held out together.

If the sum is odd, Player 1 moves forward 1 space. If the sum is even, Player 2 moves forward 1 space.

The first player to reach the finish wins!

Say • Can someone find 1 Corinthians 9:24 in the Bible and read it aloud? [*Pause for a volunteer to read.*] In today's Bible story, Paul said that being a Christian is like running a race. I can't wait to find out more!

Session starter (10 minutes)

Option 1: You too?

Encourage kids to mingle around the room. Call out a category such as "favorite ice cream." Kids should find others who share their interest and form a group.

Allow kids to move around for 30 to 60 seconds. Then call out another category: birthday month, type of pet, favorite day of the week, favorite school subject, eye color, and so forth. It's OK if a kid doesn't have a group for a certain category. Continue to play as time allows.

Say • Today we are going to learn about how God groups people together to do His work of telling people about Jesus.

Option 2: Special delivery

- masking tape or painter's tape
- paper
- envelopes, 1 per kid
- cardboard boxes or other containers, 2

Mark a start line and a turn-around line on the floor, about eight feet apart. Position each cardboard box at the turn-around line. Fold paper into each envelope and seal closed.

Form two teams. Instruct each team to line up at the start line. Give an envelope to each player. Explain that players will take turns carrying the envelope to the "mailbox" (cardboard box) and dropping it inside. Inform players that they must carry the envelope between their knees. They may not use their hands to carry the envelope.

If a player drops the envelope as he carries it, he should go back to the start line and try again. The first team to deliver all of its envelopes wins.

Say • Raise your hand if you've ever written and mailed a letter. Today's Bible story is about a message Paul wrote in a letter to a church in Corinth.

Transition to large group

Large Group LEADER

Session Title: Church Responsibility
Bible Passage: 1 Corinthians 1–16
Big Picture Question: What is the purpose of the church? The church
exists to worship God, teach believers, and make disciples of Jesus.
Key Passage: Revelation 22:12-13
Unit Christ Connection: Jesus is making all things new.

• room decorations

Tip: Select
decorations that fit
your ministry and
budget.

Suggested Theme Decorating Ideas: Decorate your
classroom to look like an art studio. Hang a paint-splattered
sheet as a backdrop. Arrange cups or buckets of art supplies
on a table and position an easel at the front of the room.
Post colorful artwork on a focal wall. Consider framing and
hanging this unit's Bible story pictures on a focal wall.

Countdown

• countdown video

Show the countdown video as your kids arrive, and set it to
end as large group time begins.

Introduce the session (3 minutes)

• leader attire
• paintbrush
• large piece of paper
• tape
• markers

*[Large Group Leader enters wearing khaki pants and a
white shirt. A paintbrush is tucked behind his or her ear.
Leader carries a large piece of paper and tapes it to the
wall or drapes it across a table.]*

Leader • Ah! A blank canvas! I just love a blank canvas,
don't you? The possibilities for creating seem endless!
You know, I've been an artist for a few years and I might
not be the best at it, but I sure have a lot of fun.

Welcome, everyone. I'm so glad to see you. Say, would
you like to help me create a masterpiece? I've decided
that as we study the Bible together over the next few

weeks, I'd like to create a mural to help us remember our time together. Today we are going to learn about the church. Does anyone want to come up here and draw something that reminds them of church? Maybe a little church building or a Bible? Oh, thank you!

Provide markers and choose a few volunteers to draw simple pictures anywhere on the large piece of paper.

Timeline map (1 minute)

• Timeline Map
• Bible Story Picture Poster (optional)

Leader •Wonderful! Well, let's get started. Like I said, our Bible story today is about the church. Let's find today's picture on our timeline map.

Point out today's Bible story picture on the timeline map, or if you framed and displayed the picture on the wall, point it out for kids to see.

Leader •I see a man standing in front of a group of people, and it looks like he is reading a letter.

Big picture question (1 minute)

Leader •Do you know that people have been meeting together as the church for about two thousand years? Have you ever wondered why people meet together as the church? That's the question we will answer in our Bible story: *What is the purpose of the church?*

Tell the Bible story (10 minutes)

• "Church Responsibility" video
• Bibles, 1 per kid
• Bible Story Picture Slide or Poster
• Big Picture Question Slide or Poster

Open your Bible to 1 Corinthians 1 and tell the Bible story in your own words, or show the Bible story video "Church Responsibility."

Leader •Have you ever thought about why you come to church? Or why the people at church do what they do? God would not be pleased if believers never met together, and He would not be pleased if we met together

Tip: A Bible story script is provided at the beginning of every session. You may use it to guide you as you prepare to teach the Bible story in your own words. For a shorter version of the Bible story, read only the bolded text.

but wasted our time by doing nothing. God has a special purpose for the church. ***What is the purpose of the church? The church exists to worship God, teach believers, and make disciples of Jesus.***

That's our big picture question and answer. When we meet together as believers—as the church—we meet to worship God. The church helps believers learn about God and the Bible. And the church exists to make disciples of Jesus. That means that telling unbelievers about Jesus and leading them to believe in Jesus and repent of their sins.

Making disciples also means helping believers learn to love and trust Jesus more so that they will "run the race" well. Paul spent a lot of time meeting with believers and encouraging them to keep following Jesus. He gave them instructions about how Christians should live. We want to honor God with our actions and attitudes because we love Him and are thankful that Jesus saved us.

We don't do good things and make right choices to convince God to let us into heaven. We do good things and make right choices because He has already promised us eternal life with Him! When we trust in Jesus as Lord and Savior, God forgives our sins and welcomes us into His family forever.

The Gospel: God's Plan for Me (optional)

Using Scripture and the guide provided, explain to boys and girls how to become a Christian. Tell kids how they can respond, and provide counselors to speak with each kid individually. Guide counselors to use open-ended questions to allow kids to determine the direction of the conversation.

Encourage boys and girls to ask their parents, small group leaders, or other adults any questions they may have about becoming a Christian.

Key passage (5 minutes)

• Key Passage Slide or Poster
• "Alpha Omega" song

Show the key passage poster and lead boys and girls to read Revelation 22:12-13. Create motions for key words to help kids memorize the first. Suggestions:

- *Look*—Hold hand flat across forehead and look around.
- *quickly*—Pump arms as if running quickly.
- *with Me*—Point to self.
- *to repay*—Reach hand out to others as if distributing something.
- *Alpha*—Hold fingertips together to form an *A*.
- *Omega*—Form an *O* with your hands.
- *First*—Point to your left.
- *Last*—Point to your right.
- *Beginning*—Point in front of you.
- *End*—Point behind you.

Leader • Jesus said these words, and John wrote them in the Book of Revelation. Jesus is coming again soon!

Guide kids to sing "Alpha Omega" together.

Discussion starter video (4 minutes)

• "Unit 36 Session 1" discussion starter video

Leader • Paul said that living life as a Christian is like running a race. Have any of you ever run an actual race? What did you do to get ready for the race? Watch this.

Show the "Unit 36 Session 1" video. Lead kids to discuss ways a runner should get ready for a race. (*rest, stretching, eating nutritious foods, and so forth*)

Leader • Paul gave the believers in Corinth some instructions for how to live. Through the Bible, God gives us rules for how to live as people who love Jesus. We obey God's rules not so that He will accept us—because He already does—but because He knows what is best for us so we can finish the work He has for us.

Sing (4 minutes)

• "Glorious Day" song

Leader • In a way, we are running a race until Jesus comes back. One day Jesus will come back. He promised that He will, and He always keeps His promises. That day will be a glorious day! Let's sing.

Lead kids in a short time of worship. Sing the song "Glorious Day" together.

Prayer (2 minutes)

• sticky notes
• markers

Leader • Thanks for coming, everyone. Before you go to your small groups, let's pray. When we pray, God listens. Is there anything you would like to pray about?

Give each kid a sticky note and a marker. Instruct kids to write about or draw a picture of something they would like to pray for. When kids finish, invite them to post their sticky notes to the mural page. Then lead the group in a brief time of prayer.

Dismiss to small groups

The Gospel: God's Plan for Me

Ask kids if they have ever heard the word *gospel*. Clarify that the word *gospel* means "good news." It is the message about Christ, the kingdom of God, and salvation. Use the following guide to share the gospel with kids.

God rules. Explain to kids that the Bible tells us God created everything, and He is in charge of everything. Invite a volunteer to read Genesis 1:1 from the Bible. Read Revelation 4:11 or Colossians 1:16-17 aloud and explain what these verses mean.

We sinned. Tell kids that since the time of Adam and Eve, everyone has chosen to disobey God. (Romans 3:23) The Bible calls this sin. Because God is holy, God cannot be around sin. Sin separates us from God and deserves God's punishment of death. (Romans 6:23)

God provided. Choose a child to read John 3:16 aloud. Say that God sent His Son, Jesus, the perfect solution to our sin problem, to rescue us from the punishment we deserve. It's something we, as sinners, could never earn on our own. Jesus alone saves us. Read and explain Ephesians 2:8-9.

Jesus gives. Share with kids that Jesus lived a perfect life, died on the cross for our sins, and rose again. Because Jesus gave up His life for us, we can be welcomed into God's family for eternity. This is the best gift ever! Read Romans 5:8; 2 Corinthians 5:21; or 1 Peter 3:18.

We respond. Tell kids that they can respond to Jesus. Read Romans 10:9-10,13. Review these aspects of our response: Believe in your heart that Jesus alone saves you through what He's already done on the cross. Repent, turning from self and sin to Jesus. Tell God and others that your faith is in Jesus.

Offer to talk with any child who is interested in responding to Jesus.

Small Group LEADER

Session Title: Church Responsibility
Bible Passage: 1 Corinthians 1–16
Big Picture Question: What is the purpose of the church? The church exists to worship God, teach believers, and make disciples of Jesus.
Key Passage: Revelation 22:12-13
Unit Christ Connection: Jesus is making all things new.

Key passage activity (5 minutes)

- Key Passage Poster
- red marker
- blue marker
- green marker
- paper

Form three teams of kids. Assign each team a color: red, blue, or green. Instruct teams to line up at one end of the room. Give the first player in each line a marker in his team's color. Show the key passage poster and review the key passage with kids. Then hide or cover the poster.

Explain that when you call out a color, the player holding that marker should run to the paper and write the first word of the key passage. His team may help him if he doesn't remember the word. When he returns to his team, he should give the marker to the next player and move to the end of the line.

Call out colors in a random order, allowing kids to take turns writing the next word in the key passage. Gently correct any mistakes. When kids finish, lead the group to say the key passage together, or prompt each team to read only the words written in its assigned color.

Say • While we wait for Jesus to return, we should meet with other believers. Together, believers make up the church. *What is the purpose of the church? The church exists to worship God, teach believers, and make disciples of Jesus.*

Bible story review & Bible skills (10 minutes)

• Bibles, 1 per kid
• Small Group Visual Pack

Option: Retell or review the Bible story using the bolded text of the Bible story script.

Give each kid a Bible. Guide boys and girls to find the Book of First Corinthians. Remind kids that Paul wrote this book as a letter to the church in Corinth. Paul had started a church there, and he wrote a letter to tell them many things about how to follow Jesus.

Ask the following review questions.

1. What did Paul compare to living for Jesus? (*running a race, 1 Cor. 9:24*)
2. What prize do believers get? (*a crown that will last forever, 1 Cor. 9:25*)
3. Who gives believers spiritual gifts? (*the Holy Spirit; 1 Cor. 12:1-6,11*)
4. What are some examples of spiritual gifts? (*wisdom, knowledge, faith; 1 Cor. 12:7-10*)
5. How did Paul describe love? (*patient, kind, not quick to get angry, and so forth; 1 Cor. 13:4-7*)
6. What did Paul say is the most important thing? (*the gospel, 1 Cor. 15:1-3*)
7. **What is the purpose of the church? The church exists to worship God, teach believers, and make disciples of Jesus.**

Say •Jesus' mission for the church is for believers to come together to worship God and to share the gospel. When we believe the gospel and trust in Jesus, God forgives our sin and we can be with Him forever.

If you choose to review with boys and girls how to become a Christian, explain that kids are welcome to speak with you or another teacher if they have questions.

- **God rules.** God created and is in charge of everything. (Gen. 1:1; Rev. 4:11; Col. 1:16-17)
- **We sinned.** Since Adam and Eve, everyone has chosen to disobey God. (Rom. 3:23; 6:23)

- **God provided.** God sent His Son, Jesus, to rescue us from the punishment we deserve. (John 3:16; Eph. 2:8-9)
- **Jesus gives.** Jesus lived a perfect life, died on the cross for our sins, and rose again so we can be welcomed into God's family. (Rom. 5:8; 2 Cor. 5:21; 1 Pet. 3:18)
- **We respond.** Believe that Jesus alone saves you. Repent. Tell God that your faith is in Jesus. (Rom. 10:9-10,13)

Activity choice (10 minutes)

- sticky notes
- marker

Option 1: Big picture points

Arrange kids' chairs in a circle. Write various point values on sticky notes and attach one to the underside of each chair. Instruct kids to walk around in the circle until you call "Stop!" Then each kid should sit down in a chair.

Call on one kid to pull the point card from under her chair. If she can answer the big picture question, she earns the class that number of points. She should put the note back under the chair. Play another round and call on another kid. Continue playing until kids have earned a predetermined total number of points, such as 20 points. Review the big picture question and answer again.

Say • *What is the purpose of the church? The church exists to worship God, teach believers, and make disciples of Jesus.*

- "Paper Church Building" (enhanced CD)
- scissors
- glue
- markers or watercolor paint

Option 2: Make a paper church building

Give each kid a paper church building template. Guide each kid to cut out the square along the dotted line. Follow the instructions to make a paper church building:

1. Fold and unfold along each line to form 16 squares.

2. Cut along the bold black lines.
3. Apply glue to the shaded area in box #1. Pull square A over the glue in box #1.
4. Repeat with box #2 and square B.
5. Apply glue to the shaded area in box #3. Pull square C over the glue.
6. Repeat with box #4 and square D.

Provide markers or watercolor paint for kids to decorate their buildings. Suggest they draw a cross on the building to indicate that it represents a church. Kids may also cut doors or windows into their paper churches.

Say • The church is made up of people who worship Jesus together. Sometimes believers meet together in a church building, but sometimes they meet in a house, school, gymnasium, or even a movie theater!

• *What is the purpose of the church? The church exists to worship God, teach believers, and make disciples of Jesus.*

Journal and prayer (5 minutes)

• pencils
• journals
• Bibles
• Journal Page, 1 per kid (enhanced CD)
• "Church Anagrams" activity page, 1 per kid

Distribute journal pages and pencils.

Say • Sketch a picture to help you remember one of the things a church exists to do: to worship God, to teach believers, and to make disciples of Jesus.

Allow time for kids to journal quietly. Close the group in prayer, thanking God for the church. Ask that God would help believers get along and work together for His glory.

As time allows, lead kids to complete the activity page "Church Anagrams." Explain that an *anagram* is a word or phrase made by changing the order of the letters in another word or phrase. Challenge boys and girls to straighten out the anagrams about why the church exists. (*worship God, teach believers, make disciples of Jesus*)

Leader BIBLE STUDY

In Acts 2:20, Peter describes the Day of the Lord with words that translate to "great," "glorious," "magnificent," "remarkable," and "awesome." The Bible says that the Day of the Lord will be a time of judgment for evildoers (Mal. 4:1) and a time of salvation and deliverance for believers (Rom. 11:26). The Day of the Lord will come quickly (Zeph. 1:14).

So imagine getting word that the Day of the Lord had already come. This is what happened to the church at Thessalonica. Some were convinced that they had missed Jesus' second coming, and they stopped working. But the Day of the Lord had not yet come.

Paul wrote to the Thessalonian church to address this misunderstanding and to encourage the believers in their faith. Paul reminded the believers that no one knows when Jesus will return. Only God Himself knows. Believers must continue to work hard—doing God's work and providing for themselves—until the moment Jesus comes. Paul even commanded the believers to stay away from people who lived irresponsibly.

Like many early Christians, the believers at Thessalonica faced persecution for their faith. Paul encouraged them not to fall away. He told them to stand strong in what they believed about Jesus. He encouraged them to "not grow weary in doing good" (2 Thess. 3:13). Life was probably difficult for the new believers, and Paul assured them that God would reward those who are faithful to Him and punish those who are against Him. (2 Thess. 1:5-7)

Paul prayed that the gospel would spread quickly, and he asked the church to pray as well. He prayed that in the midst of confusion and persecution, the Lord would give them peace.

As you teach, help kids grasp the main ideas behind Paul's letter. No one knows when Jesus will return except God Himself. Believers can stand firm through persecution and live in peace because on the great and glorious Day of the Lord, unbelievers will be punished for their sin and those who trust in Jesus will be saved.

Older Kids BIBLE STUDY OVERVIEW

Session Title: Christ's Return Is Anticipated
Bible Passage: 2 Thessalonians 1–3
Big Picture Question: When will Jesus return to earth? No one knows when Jesus will return except God Himself.
Key Passage: Revelation 22:12-13
Unit Christ Connection: Jesus is making all things new.

Small Group Opening

Large Group Leader

Small Group Leader

Additional suggestions for specific groups are available at *gospelproject.com/kids/additional-resources*.

For free online training on how to lead a group, visit *ministrygrid.com/web/thegospelproject*.

The BIBLE STORY

Christ's Return Is Anticipated
2 Thessalonians 1–3

Paul had started the church at Thessalonica (THESS uh loh NIGH kuh) about 20 years after Jesus died and rose from the dead, but Paul could not stay there long. **Paul** checked up on the church and **wrote a letter to teach the believers there and encourage them.**

Paul thanked God for the believers in Thessalonica. They loved God and each other, and their faith was growing. Even though the people in the church were being hurt or killed for believing in Jesus, they did not give up. **Paul said that God would reward them in heaven for their suffering on earth.** He said that God will punish those who don't know Him or who don't obey the gospel of Jesus.

Now Jesus had promised that He would return to earth someday. Some people were saying that He already had, that the Day of the Lord had come. **Paul told the believers that this was not true;** Jesus had not yet come. **No one knows exactly when Jesus is coming back except God Himself.**

Paul encouraged the believers to stand strong in their faith. He wrote in his letter, "God has chosen to save you." **Then Paul prayed for them**: "May our Lord Jesus Christ Himself and God our Father encourage your hearts and strengthen you in every good work and word."

Paul asked the believers in Thessalonica to pray for him and the other teachers. "Pray that the Lord's message may spread quickly, and that we may be safe from people who are wicked and evil, who do not believe," he said. **Paul knew that the Lord is faithful. He trusted God to give strength and safety to His people.**

Finally, Paul gave a warning to people who were not working hard. "If anyone is not willing to work, he should not eat." Paul said this because some people in the church were not working. Not only that, they were keeping others from working hard too.

"Do not grow weary in doing good," Paul said. "May the Lord of peace Himself give you peace always in every way. The Lord be with all of you."

Christ Connection: No one knows when Jesus will return, but Christians should be ready for Him. When Jesus returns, unbelievers will be punished for their sin and those who trust Jesus as Lord and Savior will be saved.

Want to discover God's Word? Get *Bible Express*!

Invite kids to check out today's devotional to discover the hope we have that one day Jesus will return. Like Paul told the Thessalonian church, we must not grow weary doing good as we wait for Jesus. We must always be ready to tell others about the hope that is within us! (1 Peter 3:15) Order in bulk, subscribe quarterly, or purchase individually. For more information, check out *www.lifeway.com/devotionals*.

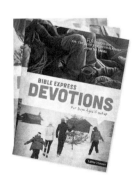

Small Group OPENING

Session Title: Christ's Return Is Anticipated
Bible Passage: 2 Thessalonians 1–3
Big Picture Question: When will Jesus return to earth? No one knows when Jesus will return except God Himself.
Key Passage: Revelation 22:12-13
Unit Christ Connection: Jesus is making all things new.

Welcome time

Greet each kid as he or she arrives. Use this time to collect the offering, fill out attendance sheets, and help new kids connect to your group. Invite kids to share one or two events they are looking forward to this week.

Activity page (5 minutes)

- "Will It Happen?" activity page, 1 per kid
- colored pencils or markers

Distribute colored pencils or markers and the "Will It Happen?" activity page. Direct each kid to color in the meter to indicate the likelihood of each event happening.

Invite kids to share their answers. Does anyone think she definitely will win a national singing contest? Does anyone think the local sports team definitely won't win every game? Why do they think that?

Say • What do you think about the last event? Will Jesus return? The Bible says He definitely will! We will learn a little more about that today.

Session starter (10 minutes)

Option 1: Mirror models
Choose two volunteers to come to the front of the room. Demonstrate three actions for them to perform. Explain that they will stand facing away from each other. When you

say go, each volunteer should perform one of the actions. Encourage the first volunteer to try to guess what they other will do. If the volunteers perform the same action, prompt the rest of the kids to cheer. If not, allow them to boo. Play several rounds.

1. Branches—Hold out your arms like branches and wiggle your fingers.
2. Boxer—Jab at the air with your fists.
3. Bounce—Bend your knees and bounce in place.

Say • Isn't it hard to guess what someone is going to do? Today we are going to hear a Bible story about some ideas people had about Jesus' return.

Option 2: Predictable results

- numbered cubes, 6
- paper
- pencils

Give each kid a pencil and a piece of paper. Explain that you will toss six numbered cubes. When you toss a cube, it could land on the number *1*, *2*, *3*, *4*, *5*, or *6*. Challenge each kid to write down which six numbers they think the cubes will land on. Use the following steps:

1. Lead kids to write down their guess for the first. Toss the cube. Was anyone correct?
2. Kids will write down another guess between one and six. Toss the second cube. Was anyone correct for both the first and second cubes?
3. Continue with the next four cubes. Was anyone able to guess the results of all six cubes in the correct order?

Say • The odds of guessing all six numbers in the correct order are 1 in more than 46,000! Do you think it is possible to predict when Jesus will return to earth? We will find out today!

Transition to large group

Large Group LEADER

Session Title: Christ's Return Is Anticipated
Bible Passage: 2 Thessalonians 1–3
Big Picture Question: When will Jesus return to earth? No one knows when Jesus will return except God Himself.
Key Passage: Revelation 22:12-13
Unit Christ Connection: Jesus is making all things new.

Countdown

• countdown video

Show the countdown video as your kids arrive, and set it to end as large group time begins.

Introduce the session (3 minutes)

• leader attire
• colored pencils
• wall mural from previous session

[Large Group Leader enters wearing khaki pants and a white shirt. A colored pencil is tucked behind his or her ear. The large mural from the previous session is displayed on a focal wall.]

Leader • Hello there! It's great to see you again. I was just admiring some of our work from last week. Here on the mural, you drew things that remind you of church. We learned about church responsibility when we studied a letter that Paul wrote to the church in Corinth.

Today we are going to hear from another letter that Paul wrote. This letter was to the church in a city called Thessalonica. Paul wrote to answer some of the people's questions. Can I have a few volunteers to come draw some question marks on our mural? That will help us remember what we are learning about today.

Provide colored pencils for a few volunteers to add to the wall mural. Thank them for their participation.

Timeline map (1 minute)

• Timeline Map
• Bible Story Picture
  Poster (optional)

Leader • Great work! Let's see if we can find today's Bible story on our timeline map.

Point out today's Bible story picture on the timeline map, or if you framed and displayed the picture on the wall, point it out for kids to see.

Leader • This is a picture of Paul writing a letter. Today's Bible story is called "Christ's Return Is Anticipated." Do you know what *anticipated* means? It means "looked forward to" or "waited for." One of the reasons Paul wrote a letter to the Thessalonians (that's what we call the people who lived in Thessalonica) is because some of them thought Jesus had already returned to earth.

Big picture question (1 minute)

Leader • That leads us to our big picture question: ***When will Jesus return to earth?*** Now that is a very good question. Let's pay close attention to our Bible story to see if we can find the answer.

Tell the Bible story (10 minutes)

• "Christ's Return Is
  Anticipated" video
• Bibles, 1 per kid
• Bible Story Picture
  Slide or Poster
• Big Picture Question
  Slide or Poster

Open your Bible to 2 Thessalonians 1 and tell the Bible story in your own words, or show the Bible story video "Christ's Return Is Anticipated."

Leader • Paul started the church in Thessalonica. Many years had passed. Paul had written a letter to the church before—First Thessalonians—and now he wrote another letter. This letter was to answer some of their questions and to explain some things that the believers were confused about.

One of the things the believers were confused about was when Jesus will return. Some people thought Jesus had already come, and they had missed Him! But that wasn't true. Paul told them Jesus had not yet come. He said that *no one knows when Jesus will return except God Himself.* That's our big picture answer. *When will Jesus return to earth? No one knows when Jesus will return except God Himself.*

Paul encouraged the church in Thessalonica not to give up. Following Jesus was not easy, but Paul said that God was going to reward them in heaven for their suffering on earth. He told them to keep working hard. Believers can look forward to the day when Jesus will return. On that day, unbelievers will be punished for their sin, and those who trust Jesus as Lord and Savior will be saved.

The Gospel: God's Plan for Me (optional)

Using Scripture and the guide provided, explain to boys and girls how to become a Christian. Tell kids how they can respond, and provide counselors to speak with each kid individually. Guide counselors to use open-ended questions to allow kids to determine the direction of the conversation.

Encourage boys and girls to ask their parents, small group leaders, or other adults any questions they may have about becoming a Christian.

Key passage (5 minutes)

• Key Passage Slide or Poster
• "Alpha Omega" song

Display the key passage poster. Guide the kids to say the key passage together. Use any hand motions you created during the last session to help kids remember the words.

Leader •When Jesus was on earth, He told His disciples that He was going to heaven but would come again. (John 14:3) Jesus is alive and in heaven today, but He promised to return. Jesus said He is coming soon. *When will Jesus return to earth? No one knows when Jesus will return except God Himself.*

Allow a volunteer to lead the class in singing "Alpha Omega."

Discussion starter video (4 minutes)

• "Unit 36 Session 2" discussion starter video

Leader • Have you ever heard anyone say that he or she knew when Jesus would return? Did you believe what that person was saying? Watch this video.

Show the "Unit 36 Session 2" video.

Leader • Some people have a lot of ideas about when Jesus will return. In Paul's day, some of the people were saying that it had already happened! The believers at the church in Thessalonica were afraid they had missed out! But Paul told them it simply wasn't true.

When will Jesus return to earth? No one knows when Jesus will return except God Himself.

Guide boys and girls to spend a minute or two discussing silly or outrageous claims they have heard. How can we tell fact from fiction?

Remind kids that the Bible is God's Word, and everything in the Bible is true. We can trust the answers we find in the Bible. We can pray and ask God to help us trust Him even when there are things we do not understand.

Sing (4 minutes)

• "Glorious Day" song

Leader • People may try to guess when Jesus will return, but no one knows except God Himself. We should always be ready. When Jesus does come, what a glorious day that will be! Do you know what I mean when I saw the word *glorious*? Some words that have similar meanings are *beautiful, dazzling, delightful, grand, great, marvelous,* and *wonderful*! Wow. Will you sing with me?

Lead kids in singing "O Glorious Day."

Prayer (2 minutes)

• sticky notes
• markers

Leader • We don't know when Jesus will return, but we should be ready. Jesus said that He is coming soon, so we need to tell our friends and everyone we meet the good news about Jesus. We can work hard as we wait for Him.

Give each kid a sticky note and a marker. Instruct kids to write about or draw a picture of something they would like to pray for. When kids finish, invite them to post their sticky notes to the mural page. Then lead the group in a brief time of prayer.

Dismiss to small groups

The Gospel: God's Plan for Me

Ask kids if they have ever heard the word *gospel*. Clarify that the word *gospel* means "good news." It is the message about Christ, the kingdom of God, and salvation. Use the following guide to share the gospel with kids.

God rules. Explain to kids that the Bible tells us God created everything, and He is in charge of everything. Invite a volunteer to read Genesis 1:1 from the Bible. Read Revelation 4:11 or Colossians 1:16-17 aloud and explain what these verses mean.

We sinned. Tell kids that since the time of Adam and Eve, everyone has chosen to disobey God. (Romans 3:23) The Bible calls this sin. Because God is holy, God cannot be around sin. Sin separates us from God and deserves God's punishment of death. (Romans 6:23)

God provided. Choose a child to read John 3:16 aloud. Say that God sent His Son, Jesus, the perfect solution to our sin problem, to rescue us from the punishment we deserve. It's something we, as sinners, could never earn on our own. Jesus alone saves us. Read and explain Ephesians 2:8-9.

Jesus gives. Share with kids that Jesus lived a perfect life, died on the cross for our sins, and rose again. Because Jesus gave up His life for us, we can be welcomed into God's family for eternity. This is the best gift ever! Read Romans 5:8; 2 Corinthians 5:21; or 1 Peter 3:18.

We respond. Tell kids that they can respond to Jesus. Read Romans 10:9-10,13. Review these aspects of our response: Believe in your heart that Jesus alone saves you through what He's already done on the cross. Repent, turning from self and sin to Jesus. Tell God and others that your faith is in Jesus.

Offer to talk with any child who is interested in responding to Jesus.

Small Group LEADER

Session Title: Christ's Return Is Anticipated
Bible Passage: 2 Thessalonians 1–3
Big Picture Question: When will Jesus return to earth? No one knows when Jesus will return except God Himself.
Key Passage: Revelation 22:12-13
Unit Christ Connection: Jesus is making all things new.

Key passage activity (5 minutes)

- Key Passage Poster
- paper plates
- markers

Write each word of the key passage on a separate paper plate. Arrange the plates facedown in a grid. Invite kids to take turns flipping over the plates to find the words of the verses in order. If a player turns over a plate that does not contain the next word, he should position it facedown and allow the next player a turn.

As kids collect the words in order, they should arrange them faceup on the floor. When the plates are all faceup, encourage kids to say the key passage together.

Say • Jesus has not returned yet, but He said in the Book of Revelation that He is coming soon. While we wait for His return, we can work together with other believers to tell others about Him.

Bible story review & Bible skills (10 minutes)

- Bibles, 1 per kid
- Small Group Visual Pack
- numbered cube

Option: Retell or review the Bible story using the bolded text of the Bible story script.

Form two teams. Teams will take turns answering review questions. For each correct answer, the team will roll a numbered cube to determine how many points the team earns. For an incorrect answer, give the other team a chance to answer. Sample review questions:

1. To whom did Paul write 2 Thessalonians? (*to the church in Thessalonica, to the Thessalonians;*

2 Thess. 1:1)

2. True or false: The believers in Thessalonica loved each other and loved God. (*true, 2 Thess. 1:3*)

3. What did Paul say God will do for those who follow Him? (*God will reward them, 2 Thess. 1:7*)

4. What did Paul say God will do for those who do not follow Him? (*God will punish them; 2 Thess. 1:6,8*)

Say •Paul wrote two letters to the church in Thessalonica. We find them in our Bible as 1 Thessalonians and 2 Thessalonians. Paul wrote to answer questions about when Jesus will return. ***When will Jesus return to earth? No one knows when Jesus will return except God Himself.*** But Christians should be ready for Him. When Jesus returns, unbelievers will be punished for their sin and those who trust in Jesus as Lord and Savior will be saved.

If you choose to review with boys and girls how to become a Christian, explain that kids are welcome to speak with you or another teacher if they have questions.

- **God rules.** God created and is in charge of everything. (Gen. 1:1; Rev. 4:11; Col. 1:16-17)
- **We sinned.** Since Adam and Eve, everyone has chosen to disobey God. (Rom. 3:23; 6:23)
- **God provided.** God sent His Son, Jesus, to rescue us from the punishment we deserve. (John 3:16; Eph. 2:8-9)
- **Jesus gives.** Jesus lived a perfect life, died on the cross for our sins, and rose again so we can be welcomed into God's family. (Rom. 5:8; 2 Cor. 5:21; 1 Pet. 3:18)
- **We respond.** Believe that Jesus alone saves you. Repent. Tell God that your faith is in Jesus. (Rom. 10:9-10,13)

Activity choice (10 minutes)

Option 1: Has it happened?

Explain that you will describe an event or discovery. Kids should jump up and down if they think it has happened, or they should sit on the floor if they think it has not happened.

1. An astronomer measured how fast light travels. (*happened in 1676*)
2. A doctor discovered a medicine to prevent all types of sicknesses. (*has not happened*)
3. A basketball player made a basket from more than 109 feet away from the goal. (*happened in 2013*)
4. A woman grew a species of plant that will never die. (*has not happened*)
5. Animals were safely sent into space. (*happened in 1960*)
6. A man did 1,868 one arm push-ups in one hour. (*happened in 1993*)
7. People have built and lived in cities on the planet Mars. (*has not happened*)
8. Jesus has returned. (*has not happened*)

Say • Some of the people in Thessalonica said that Jesus had already returned. But Paul wrote a letter to the believers to say that it wasn't true. Jesus' return had not yet happened. Today, we are still waiting for Jesus to come back. As we wait, we should be ready.

• *When will Jesus return to earth? No one knows when Jesus will return except God Himself.*

Option 2: Create a calendar

• paper
• rules
• markers

Give each kid a piece of paper, a ruler, and a marker.

Demonstrate how to position the paper in a landscape orientation and draw six vertical lines, 1½ inches apart. Kids should now have seven columns. Guide them to label the columns with the days of the week to create a seven-day calendar. Ask kids to write in any activities they are looking forward to doing or events they'd like to go to this week.

Encourage boys and girls to note specific times that they wake up, eat lunch, have soccer practice or dance lessons, go to bed, and so forth. Allow a few volunteers to share their schedules with the rest of the group.

Say • We can make plans for the future, and many of the things we plan for will happen—but sometimes they don't. One thing we can be sure will happen is that Jesus will return. Jesus promised He would come back, and He always keeps His promises!

• *When will Jesus return to earth? No one knows when Jesus will return except God Himself.*

Journal and prayer (5 minutes)

- pencils
- journals
- Bibles
- Journal Page, 1 per kid (enhanced CD)
- "On the Schedule" activity page, 1 per kid

Distribute journal pages and pencils. Suggest kids list or draw pictures of things they are looking forward to that they might not get to do if Jesus were to return tomorrow.

Assure boys and girls that Jesus' return will be so much better than anything on earth. Open your Bible to Isaiah 65:17 and invite a volunteer to read the verse aloud.

Say • The Bible says that God will make a new creation—a new heavens and a new earth. When that happens, we won't even remember or think about the things that happen to us now.

As time allows, lead kids to complete the activity page "On the Schedule." Kids will use the coordinates to find the letters to solve the puzzle. For example, B5 indicates row B, column 5: the letter *N*. (*No one knows when Jesus will return except God Himself.*)

Leader BIBLE STUDY

The apostle John wrote the Book of Revelation from the island of Patmos. Patmos was an island where the Romans often exiled prisoners. John was likely sent to Patmos as a prisoner, arrested for preaching the gospel. Introduce kids to the Book of Revelation—the last book of the Bible and a book that tells about things that will happen in the future. A glimpse of the future kingdom of God gives believers hope and compels them to remain faithful to Christ.

The Book of Revelation opens with John's description of a vision. In the vision, Jesus warned seven local churches. In most cases, Jesus commended the church for their good work, warned them about the areas in which they needed correction, and urged them to return to Him. Each time, Jesus promised to reward those who remain faithful to Him.

Jesus loves the church. The Church is made up of people who have trusted in Jesus, who are committed to one another, and who meet together to worship Jesus and share the gospel. Jesus loves the church as His bride. (See Eph. 5:25-27; Rev. 19:7-9.) Jesus' message to seven local churches called them to turn away from their sin and remain faithful to Him. The Lord is slow to anger (Ex. 34-6-7) and patient, wanting everyone to repent (2 Pet. 3:9).

Help kids understand some of the problems the early churches faced. They did not love like they should, they believed false teaching and did wrong things, and they were lukewarm—useless to the cause of Christ. Churches still face these problems today. We can pray for our churches to be faithful, effective instruments in spreading the gospel.

Jesus is "the Alpha and the Omega" (Rev. 1:8). In the Greek alphabet, *alpha* is the first letter and *omega* is the last. Jesus is the A to Z. Jesus is the beginning and the end, but not just those; He is everything in-between. Jesus made all things. (John 1:3) He is in control of all things. He holds all things together. (Col. 1:17) And He is coming back someday!

Older Kids BIBLE STUDY OVERVIEW

Session Title: God's Warning to Seven Churches
Bible Passage: Revelation 1–3
Big Picture Question: What did Jesus tell the churches about Himself?
   Jesus is the Alpha and the Omega—the beginning and the end.
Key Passage: Revelation 22:12-13
Unit Christ Connection: Jesus is making all things new.

Small Group Opening

Large Group Leader

Small Group Leader

Additional suggestions for specific groups are available at *gospelproject.com/kids/additional-resources*.

For free online training on how to lead a group, visit *ministrygrid.com/web/thegospelproject*.

The BIBLE STORY

God's Warning to Seven Churches
Revelation 1–3

Like many believers, the apostle John faced suffering and persecution for telling people about Jesus. **John was on the island of Patmos** (PAT muhs) **when he had a vision.** John saw Jesus and seven gold lampstands. The seven lampstands were the seven churches. **Jesus told John to write down the things he saw and send the message to the seven churches.** John obeyed Jesus. **These are the messages to the seven churches.**

"To the church in Ephesus (EF uh suhs)**: I know what you do. You work hard and do not give up. You do not accept people who do evil things. But I have this against you: You do not love well like you did when you first believed. Turn back and love like you used to.**

"Everyone should pay attention to this message from the Spirit. Jesus will reward believers who are faithful.

"To the church in Smyrna (SMUHR nuh)**: I know that you are poor and are suffering, but really you are rich! I know that people insult you. You may face prison or death, but do not be afraid.**

"Everyone should pay attention to this message from the Spirit. Jesus will reward believers who are faithful.

"To the church in Pergamum (PUHR guh muhm)**: I know that you live in a place where people do evil things. But you are faithful to Me, and you tell others about Me even when it is hard. But not everyone in the church is doing the right thing.** Some people are living like those who do not believe. **Turn away from your sin and turn back to Me!**

"Everyone should pay attention to this message from the Spirit. Jesus will reward believers who are faithful.

"To the church in Thyatira (THIGH uh TIGH ruh)**: I know what you do. I know about your love, faithfulness, and service. You do not give up. But there is a wicked woman with you who teaches things that are not true, and some of you believe her.** I will punish her and those who follow her teaching. **Many of you do not follow her, and to you I say, keep believing the truth until I come.** Everyone should pay attention to this message from the Spirit. Jesus will reward believers who are faithful.

"**To the church in Sardis** (SAHR diss)**:** I know what you do. People think you are alive, but you are actually dead. **You used to have a strong faith, but now you are weak.** You do not live as you should. **Wake up! Be ready for My return. Turn from your sin and remember the gospel.** Turn back to the Lord and live for Him.

"Everyone should pay attention to this message from the Spirit. Jesus will reward believers who are faithful.

"**To the church in Philadelphia** (FIL uh DEL fih uh)**:** I know what you do. **You are a small church, but you listen to Me and obey My word. I have opened the door for you to enter My kingdom. I am coming soon. Be ready and keep believing.** Everyone should pay attention to this message from the Spirit. Jesus will reward believers who are faithful.

"**To the church in Laodicea** (lay AHD ih SEE uh)**:** I know what you do. **You are not hot or cold, so you are not good for anything. I will spit you out of My mouth!** You think you are rich, but you are actually poor, blind, and naked. Come to me, and I will make you rich. I will make you see, and I will put clothes on you.

"**I am here! I stand at the door and knock. If you hear my voice and open the door, I will come in and eat with you, and you will eat with Me.** Everyone should pay attention to this message from the Spirit. Jesus will reward believers who are faithful."

Christ Connection: Jesus loves the church. His message to seven local churches called them to turn away from their sin and remain faithful to Him. Jesus saves sinners and changes them to be like Him.

Want to discover God's Word? Get *Bible Express*!

Invite kids to check out today's devotional to discover that David described obeying God's commandments as a delight. (Psalm 40:8) Some of the churches mentioned in Jesus' warning forgot the joy and love they first felt when they became followers of Jesus, but it wasn't too late for them to repent! Order in bulk, subscribe quarterly, or purchase individually. For more information, check out *www.lifeway.com/devotionals*.

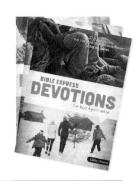

Small Group OPENING

Session Title: God's Warning to Seven Churches
Bible Passage: Revelation 1–3
Big Picture Question: What did Jesus tell the churches about Himself?
 Jesus is the Alpha and the Omega—the beginning and the end.
Key Passage: Revelation 22:12-13
Unit Christ Connection: Jesus is making all things new.

Welcome time

Greet each kid as he or she arrives. Use this time to collect the offering, fill out attendance sheets, and help new kids connect to your group. Invite kids to think about some warnings they might have heard this week. For example: stop signs, caution tape, verbal warnings from parents, and so forth. Ask kids to share what happens when we ignore a warning. (*We could get hurt.*) Explain that warnings are meant to keep us safe.

Activity page (5 minutes)

- "Seven Churches" activity page, 1 per kid
- pencils

Give boys and girls the "Seven Churches" activity page. Challenge them to find the seven church buildings hidden in the picture.

Say • Today's Bible story is a message from Jesus to some churches. How many churches do you think this message is for? (*seven*)

Session starter (10 minutes)

- index cards
- marker

Option 1: Start and finish

Prepare to play partner charades by writing the following events on separate index cards: *playing a basketball game, mowing the lawn, talking on the phone, doing the dishes, reading a book*, and *getting a haircut*. If your group is large, consider listing a few more events that have clear beginnings and endings.

1. Invite two volunteers to draw an index card.
2. The first volunteer should act out the beginning of the event.
3. The second volunteer should act out the end of the event.
4. Encourage the rest of the group to guess what the volunteers are acting out.

Example: When talking on the phone the first player might begin by picking up a pretend phone and mouthing a conversation. The second volunteer should mouth a brief conversation and then hang up the phone.

After kids guess, allow another pair to act out an event.

Say • In today's Bible story, Jesus said, "I am the beginning and the end." What do you think He meant by that? We will soon find out!

Option 2: What's in common?

• sets of 7 common objects (paper clips, rubber bands, toy cars, and so forth)

Mix up the objects and distribute them among the kids. Ask them to work together to study the objects and figure out what they all have in common. What are the objects used for? Who typically uses them?

Encourage boys and girls to sort the objects and count them. (*There are seven of each object.*)

Say • Today's Bible story is about a message Jesus gave to seven churches in Asia. The seven churches were at Ephesus, Smyrna, Pergamum, Thyatira, Sardis, Philadelphia, and Laodicea.

Transition to large group

Large Group LEADER

Session Title: God's Warning to Seven Churches
Bible Passage: Revelation 1–3
Big Picture Question: What did Jesus tell the churches about Himself?
Jesus is the Alpha and the Omega—the beginning and the end.
Key Passage: Revelation 22:12-13
Unit Christ Connection: Jesus is making all things new.

Countdown

• countdown video

Show the countdown video as your kids arrive, and set it to end as large group time begins.

Introduce the session (3 minutes)

• leader attire
• large crayons
• wall mural from previous sessions

[Large Group Leader enters wearing khaki pants and a white shirt. A large crayon is tucked behind his or her ear. The large mural from the previous sessions is displayed on a focal wall.]

Leader • Hi, everyone! Thank you for all of your help so far with this mural. It looks great. I see some things that remind us of the church, and I see a lot of question marks!

Are you ready to add to it? Today's Bible story is about God's warning to seven churches. Can I have seven volunteers come up and draw the number 7?

Provide crayons for kids to draw. Encourage them to draw the number 7 in several areas of the mural.

Timeline map (1 minute)

• Timeline Map
• Bible Story Picture Poster (optional)

Leader • Wonderful! The last two Bible stories we heard were from letters Paul wrote to churches. Now, Paul didn't write the story we are going to hear today. The apostle John wrote this story.

Point out today's Bible story picture on the timeline map, or if you framed and displayed the picture on wall, point it out for kids to see.

Leader • Here is a picture of John, and these are lampstands. How many lampstands are there? One, two, three, four, five, six, seven!

Big picture question (1 minute)

Leader • The lampstands in the Bible story picture represent seven churches. You see, John was on an island when Jesus gave him a message. Jesus told John to write down what he saw and to give the message to the seven churches. And that's what John did.

The question we are trying to answer today—our big picture question—is this: ***What did Jesus tell the churches about Himself?*** I think we will need to listen to the Bible story to find out!

Tell the Bible story (10 minutes)

• "God's Warning to Seven Churches" video
• Bibles, 1 per kid
• Bible Story Picture Slide or Poster
• Big Picture Question Slide or Poster

Open your Bible to Revelation 1 and tell the Bible story in your own words, or show the Bible story video "God's Warning to Seven Churches."

Leader • Jesus sure had a lot to say to these churches. Jesus told John to write these messages on a scroll and send them to the churches. Jesus knew what was going on in each church, and He told them what they were doing well and what they needed to repent of, or stop doing.

The things the believers were doing in those churches long ago are still things believers sometimes do in churches today. We can learn from Jesus' messages to the seven churches.

First, Jesus told the churches something about Himself. He said that ***Jesus is the Alpha and the Omega—the*** *beginning and the end.* Say that with me. ***What did Jesus tell the churches about Himself? Jesus is the Alpha and the Omega—the beginning and the end.*** If you don't know Greek, don't worry! I will tell you that *Alpha* is the first letter of the Greek alphabet, and *Omega* is the last letter. Think of Alpha and Omega as A and Z. Jesus was saying, "I am the A and the Z." Jesus said that He has always existed, He is alive today, and He will come again. [*See Rev. 1:8.*]

In His messages, Jesus told the church in Ephesus to love Him like the used to. If you are a Christian, do you remember when you first believed in Jesus? Were you really excited to go to church? Have you always felt that way, or do you ever feel like you don't want to read your Bible or pray? The believers in the Ephesian church were feeling like that. Jesus told the believers to turn back to Him and love Him like they first did.

He told the church in Pergamum that they were faithful to Him. The believers there told others about Jesus even when it was hard. But some people in the church did evil things, and Jesus warned them to turn back to Him.

Jesus told the believers in the church at Sardis to get ready for His return. On the outside, they looked alive and strong. But Jesus knew their faith was weak. He told them to remember the gospel and turn away from their sin.

Jesus was happy with the church in Philadelphia. The believers there listened to Jesus and obeyed Him. He encouraged them and told them to be ready for His return. He told them to keep believing in Him.

Jesus said that everyone should pay attention to the messages for the seven churches.

The Gospel: God's Plan for Me (optional)

Using Scripture and the guide provided, explain to boys and girls how to become a Christian. Tell kids how they can respond, and provide counselors to speak with each kid individually. Guide counselors to use open-ended questions to allow kids to determine the direction of the conversation.

Encourage boys and girls to ask their parents, small group leaders, or other adults any questions they may have about becoming a Christian.

Key passage (5 minutes)

• Key Passage Slide or Poster
• "Alpha Omega" song

Show the key passage poster. Review any hand motions created in previous sessions to reinforce the key words. Lead kids to say Revelation 22:12-13 together.

Leader • Jesus said that He would reward or pay back each person according to what his or her actions deserve. He said He would punish evil and reward those who serve Him.

Invite kids to sing along to "Alpha Omega."

Discussion starter video (5 minutes)

• "Unit 36 Session 3" discussion starter video

Leader • Do you remember what Jesus said to the church at Laodicea? He said that they were lukewarm—not hot or cold. Think about hot water. People can sit in a hot bath and it heals sore and achy muscles. And cold water is refreshing when you are thirsty. But room-temperature water is yucky! Watch this.

Show the "Unit 36 Session 3" video.

Leader • Jesus said that the believers at Laodicea were lukewarm—not hot or cold. He said He would spit them out of His mouth. Jesus wanted the believers to be totally committed to Him. He didn't want them to only obey Him when they felt like it or only serve others when it was convenient. He wanted them to be all in!

Lead kids to discuss other ways Christians might be lukewarm. (*reading the Bible out of duty instead of delight, not paying attention during the worship service, not singing at church, falling asleep during prayer, and so forth*)

Sing (3 minutes)

• *"Glorious Day" song*

Leader • Jesus loves the church, and He wants believers to turn away from sin and be faithful to Him. One day, Jesus will come back to earth. He will reward believers and bring them to live with Him forever. That will be a glorious day. Let's sing.

Lead boys and girls to sing "Glorious Day."

Prayer (2 minutes)

• sticky notes
• markers

Leader • Before you go to your small groups, let's pray. Heavenly Father, thank You for the church. Thank You for working through groups of believers to spread the gospel in the whole world. God, we pray that You would help us not be lukewarm. Give us a passion to follow You our whole lives. Lead us to repent of worshiping You halfheartedly. You are our Lord and our God, and we love You. Bless our time together today. In Jesus' name, amen.

Give each kid a sticky note and a marker. Instruct kids to write about or draw a picture of something they would like to pray for. When kids finish, invite them to post their sticky notes to the mural page. Encourage kids to pray for these prayer requests this week.

Dismiss to small groups

The Gospel: God's Plan for Me

Ask kids if they have ever heard the word *gospel*. Clarify that the word *gospel* means "good news." It is the message about Christ, the kingdom of God, and salvation. Use the following guide to share the gospel with kids.

God rules. Explain to kids that the Bible tells us God created everything, and He is in charge of everything. Invite a volunteer to read Genesis 1:1 from the Bible. Read Revelation 4:11 or Colossians 1:16-17 aloud and explain what these verses mean.

We sinned. Tell kids that since the time of Adam and Eve, everyone has chosen to disobey God. (Romans 3:23) The Bible calls this sin. Because God is holy, God cannot be around sin. Sin separates us from God and deserves God's punishment of death. (Romans 6:23)

God provided. Choose a child to read John 3:16 aloud. Say that God sent His Son, Jesus, the perfect solution to our sin problem, to rescue us from the punishment we deserve. It's something we, as sinners, could never earn on our own. Jesus alone saves us. Read and explain Ephesians 2:8-9.

Jesus gives. Share with kids that Jesus lived a perfect life, died on the cross for our sins, and rose again. Because Jesus gave up His life for us, we can be welcomed into God's family for eternity. This is the best gift ever! Read Romans 5:8; 2 Corinthians 5:21; or 1 Peter 3:18.

We respond. Tell kids that they can respond to Jesus. Read Romans 10:9-10,13. Review these aspects of our response: Believe in your heart that Jesus alone saves you through what He's already done on the cross. Repent, turning from self and sin to Jesus. Tell God and others that your faith is in Jesus.

Offer to talk with any child who is interested in responding to Jesus.

Small Group LEADER

Session Title: God's Warning to Seven Churches
Bible Passage: Revelation 1–3
Big Picture Question: What did Jesus tell the churches about Himself?
   Jesus is the Alpha and the Omega—the beginning and the end.
Key Passage: Revelation 22:12-13
Unit Christ Connection: Jesus is making all things new.

Key passage activity (5 minutes)

- Key Passage Poster
- heavyweight paper
- scissors

Print a copy of the key passage poster on heavyweight paper. Cut it into seven pieces and hide them around the room. Challenge kids to find the seven pieces and put them together. Then lead them to read the key passage aloud. If time allows, hide the pieces and play again.

Say • The Book of Revelation is the last book in the Bible. John wrote this book when he was on an island, probably as a prisoner. He wrote about the things Jesus said about the future. Jesus said He is coming again soon!

Bible story review & Bible skills (10 minutes)

- Bibles, 1 per kid
- Small Group Visual Pack
- ball of yarn or string

Option: Retell or review the Bible story using the bolded text of the Bible story script.

Guide kids to stand in a circle. Give one player a ball of yarn. Tell her she may answer a review question or tell the group a fact she remembers from the Bible story. Then she should hold onto the end of the yarn and toss the ball of yarn to another player.

   The second player will tell a fact or answer a question, grab the line of yarn, and toss the ball of yarn to another player. As kids review the Bible story, they will form a yarn web. If a kid cannot think of a fact to share, encourage him to find Revelation 1–3 in a Bible. Assign him a verse to read

aloud: Revelation 1:3; 1:8; 1:10; 1:17; 2:4; 2:10; 2:29; 3:11.
Suggested review questions:

1. Who wrote the Book of Revelation? (*John, Rev. 1:1*)
2. Who was John writing to? (*to the seven churches in Asia, Rev. 1:4*)
3. What did John say Jesus will do for believers who are faithful? (*reward them; Rev. 2:7,11,17*)
4. Did the church in Ephesus love Jesus more or less than when they first loved Him? (*less, Rev. 2:4*)
5. What dangers did the church in Smyrna face? (*prison or death, Rev. 2:10*)
6. What did Jesus tell the church in Pergamum to do? (*repent, turn away from their sin and turn back to Him; Rev. 2:16*)
7. Was the church in Laodicea hot or cold? (*neither, it was lukewarm; Rev. 3:15-16*)

Say • *What did Jesus tell the churches about Himself? Jesus is the Alpha and the Omega—the beginning and the end.*

• Jesus loves the church. His message to seven local churches called them to turn away from their sin and remain faithful to Him. Jesus saves sinners and changes them to be like Him.

If you choose to review with boys and girls how to become a Christian, explain that kids are welcome to speak with you or another teacher if they have questions.

• **God rules.** God created and is in charge of everything. (Gen. 1:1; Rev. 4:11; Col. 1:16-17)
• **We sinned.** Since Adam and Eve, everyone has chosen to disobey God. (Rom. 3:23; 6:23)
• **God provided.** God sent His Son, Jesus, to rescue us from the punishment we deserve. (John 3:16; Eph. 2:8-9)

- **Jesus gives.** Jesus lived a perfect life, died on the cross for our sins, and rose again so we can be welcomed into God's family. (Rom. 5:8; 2 Cor. 5:21; 1 Pet. 3:18)
- **We respond.** Believe that Jesus alone saves you. Repent. Tell God that your faith is in Jesus. (Rom. 10:9-10,13)

Activity choice (10 minutes)

· 2 balls of different sizes or colors

Tip: If the bird can't catch the worm, add another bird to the game.

Option 1: The bird and the worm

Instruct the group to form a circle. Give the balls to two players on opposite sides of the circle. Designate which ball is the bird and which is the worm. Explain that this game is like hot potato; the balls should not be held for more than one second. Give the following instructions:

1. The object of the game is for the bird to catch the worm.
2. Both the bird and the worm move around the circle by being passed (not thrown) in any direction.
3. If a player is holding the bird, he should pass it to the player next to him who is closest to the worm. The player holding the worm should pass it to someone farther away from the bird.
4. When the bird catches the worm, everyone should say the big picture question and answer.

Say • *What did Jesus tell the churches about Himself? Jesus is the Alpha and the Omega—the beginning and the end.*

Option 2: "Knock, knock" circle

· Bible

Instruct kids to sit around a table. If your group is large, kids may sit in a circle on the floor. Demonstrate how to softly knock on the table with your knuckles. Encourage the kids to knock softly. Tap your foot to keep a consistent rhythm. Then instruct them to stop. Explain the game:

1. The first player will begin by tapping a simple four-beat rhythm, such as a slow knock–knock– knock–pause. The first player should repeat her rhythm without changing it.
2. Then the player to her left will add his rhythm. For example: knock–pause–knock–pause. He should repeat his rhythm without any changes.
3. Invite kids to add their own rhythms one at a time.

When everyone is knocking softly, allow kids to listen for a minute or two. Then point to the first player so she will stop knocking. Continue around the circle until only the last player is knocking. Then silence all the rhythms. Open your Bible to Revelation 3:20 and read the verse aloud.

Say • Jesus told the church at Laodicea that He stands at the door and knocks. The believers in the church had, in a way, pushed Jesus away. But He was waiting for them to open the door and let Him back in. Jesus said He would come in and eat with them, and they would be friends.

Journal and prayer (5 minutes)

- pencils
- journals
- Bibles
- Journal Page, 1 per kid (enhanced CD)
- "A to Z Scramble" activity page, 1 per kid

Distribute journal pages and pencils. Encourage kids to write a letter to a friend, sharing something they learned during today's Bible study.

As time allows, lead kids to complete the activity page "A to Z Scramble." Lead kids to unscramble the names of the seven churches found in Revelation 2–3. (*Ephesus, Smyrna, Pergamum, Thyatira, Sardis, Philadelphia, Laodicea*)

Kids should use the circled letters to fill in the phrase from Revelation 1:8—Jesus is the *Alpha* and the *Omega*.

Leader BIBLE STUDY

While he was a prisoner on the island of Patmos, the apostle John had an amazing vision of heaven. Jesus told John to write down everything he saw. John saw things that will happen when Jesus comes back to earth. Jesus—who entered Jerusalem humbly on a donkey—will come victoriously, riding on a white horse. His name will be on His robe and His thigh:

> KING OF KINGS
> AND LORD OF LORDS.

Satan and the evil ones will be defeated and thrown into the lake of fire. The Lord will be on His throne. Then out of heaven will come a new creation—a new heaven and a new earth. The distance and separation that exists between people and God will be no more. God will dwell with humanity. They will be His people, and He will be their God.

John described the beauty of the New City—the New Jerusalem. The streets will be pure gold, like clear glass. The foundations of the city wall will be adorned with precious stones. The city will not need the sun or the moon because God's glory will illuminate it. There will be no darkness, and nothing evil will ever come into the city.

The promised return of Christ should fill believers with hope, strengthening them to persevere through the trials of this life and remain faithful to the Lord. When Christ returns, those who trust in Him will be with Him and enjoy Him forever. God will undo every bad thing caused by sin—no more death, no more pain, no more tears.

Christ's return should also give believers a sense of urgency to share the gospel with the world. It is the power of God for salvation to everyone who believes! (Rom. 1:16) Jesus is coming soon. Amen. Come, Lord Jesus!

Older Kids BIBLE STUDY OVERVIEW

Session Title: Jesus Christ Will Return
Bible Passage: Revelation 19–22
Big Picture Question: What will we do after Jesus returns? God will live with His people, and we will enjoy Him forever.
Key Passage: Revelation 22:12-13
Unit Christ Connection: Jesus is making all things new.

U
N
I
T
36

4

Small Group Opening

Large Group Leader

Small Group Leader

Additional suggestions for specific groups are available at *gospelproject.com/kids/additional-resources*.

For free online training on how to lead a group, visit *ministrygrid.com/web/thegospelproject*.

The BIBLE STORY

Jesus Christ Will Return
Revelation 19–22

John had a vision of heaven. He heard a large crowd of people praising God and rejoicing. **In his vision, John also saw the things that would happen when Jesus comes back to earth. This is what John wrote down:**

"**I saw heaven opened, and there was a white horse. Its rider is called Faithful and True.** His eyes were like a fiery flame, and there were many crowns on His head. He wore a robe stained with blood, and His name is the Word of God. The armies that were in heaven followed Him on white horses. **And He has a name written on His robe and on His thigh:**

**KING OF KINGS
AND LORD OF LORDS.**

"**Then I saw the beast, the kings of the earth, and their armies gathered together to fight against the rider and His army. But the beast and the false prophet was captured. Both of them were thrown into the lake of fire.**

"**I saw Satan's army march across the earth.** They surrounded the camp of God's people. **But fire came down from heaven and destroyed Satan's army. And Satan was thrown into the lake of fire.**

"**Then I saw a new heaven and a new earth. The first heaven and the first earth had disappeared.** I also saw the Holy City, a new Jerusalem, coming down out of heaven from God. **I heard a loud voice from the throne, saying, 'Look! God will live with His people. They will be His people, and He will be their God. He will wipe away every tear from their eyes. Death will no longer exist. Sadness, crying, and pain will no longer exist. These things have passed away.'**

"**Then one of the angels** came and carried me to a great and high mountain. He **showed me the Holy City, new Jerusalem. The city was shining with God's glory.** The foundations of the city wall had every type of precious stone. The city street was made of pure gold, as clear as glass.

"I did not see a temple in the city because the Lord and the Lamb were the city's temple. **The city does not need the sun or the moon to shine on it. The glory of God gives light to the city, and there is no darkness. The city is safe and clean—nothing unclean and no one who does wrong things will ever come into the city.** Only those whose names are in the Lamb's book of life will enter the city. God's servants will see His face, and they will worship Him. The Lord will reign forever and ever.

"**Jesus said, 'Listen, I am coming soon! I am the Alpha and the Omega, the First and the Last, the Beginning and the End.'**

"Jesus is the One who says that all of these things will happen. He says, 'Yes, I am coming soon.'

"**Amen! Come, Lord Jesus!**"

Christ Connection: Jesus promised to come back to earth soon. When Christ returns, those who trust in Jesus will be with Him and enjoy Him forever. God will undo every bad thing caused by sin—no more death, no more pain, no more tears. Jesus is making all things new.

Want to discover God's Word? Get *Bible Express*! Invite kids to check out today's devotional to discover how we should live as we wait for Jesus to return. (Titus 2:11-13) What a glorious day that will be! Order in bulk, subscribe quarterly, or purchase individually. For more information, check out *www.lifeway.com/devotionals*.

God's Plan for the Church Is Fulfilled

Small Group OPENING

Session Title: Jesus Christ Will Return
Bible Passage: Revelation 19–22
Big Picture Question: What will we do after Jesus returns? God will live
  with His people, and we will enjoy Him forever.
Key Passage: Revelation 22:12-13
Unit Christ Connection: Jesus is making all things new.

Welcome time

Greet each kid as he or she arrives. Use this time to collect
the offering, fill out attendance sheets, and help new kids
connect to your group. Invite kids to share their best day
ever. What happened? What made that day so great?

Activity page (5 minutes)

- "No More" activity
  page, 1 per kid
- pencils

Lead boys and girls to complete the activity page "No
More." Kids will find and cross out the words from the
word list. Also guide them to cross out the letters *A*, *M*, and
O. Then lead them to write the remaining letters in order
from left to right, top to bottom. (*Jesus will return.*)

Say • Can you imagine living in a world where there is
no sin or death or crying or pain? Where evildoers,
enemies, and liars are not allowed to be? Where there
is no darkness?

Invite kids to share things or events they would be glad to
have no more of. Tell kids that Jesus will get rid of illness,
injuries, loneliness, envy, and hatred.

Say • The Bible says that one day we will live in a place
with no more of those things! One day, Jesus will
return and we will live with Him forever.

· paper
· pencils

Session starter (10 minutes)

Option 1: Alphabet search

Form groups of three or four kids. Give each group a piece of paper and a pencil. Instruct each group to choose one person to be the writer. The writer should list each letter of the alphabet down the left side of the paper.

Challenge kids to move around the classroom and try to find objects that begin with each letter of the alphabet. Instruct each group to write down the name of each object and leave the objects in their places.

Allow kids to search for several minutes. Then call everyone together. Say a few letters and invite kids to tell what objects they found. Were there any letters they did not find an object for?

Say • In today's Bible story, Jesus said that He is the Alpha and the Omega. Those are the first and last letters of the Greek alphabet—the A and Z!

· Bible
· paper
· colored pencils
· markers
· rulers

Option 2: Design your dream room

Provide art supplies for kids. Prompt them to imagine what they would like if they could have their dream bedroom. What furniture would they have? What color would the walls be painted? What toys would they have?

Invite boys and girls to draw pictures of their dream rooms. As they work, open the Bible to John 14:2-3 and read the verses aloud.

Say • When Jesus was on earth, He told His disciples that there are many rooms in His Father's house. Jesus said He would go to prepare a room for us and that He would come back. Today we will learn more about the day when Jesus will return.

Transition to large group

Large Group LEADER

Session Title: Jesus Christ Will Return
Bible Passage: Revelation 19–22
Big Picture Question: What will we do after Jesus returns? God will live with His people, and we will enjoy Him forever.
Key Passage: Revelation 22:12-13
Unit Christ Connection: Jesus is making all things new.

Countdown

• countdown video

Show the countdown video as your kids arrive, and set it to end as large group time begins.

Introduce the session (3 minutes)

• leader attire
• scarf
• wall mural from previous sessions

[Large Group Leader enters wearing khaki pants and a white shirt. Leader wears a scarf around his or her neck. The large mural from the previous sessions is displayed on a focal wall.]

Leader • You're back! I am so glad to see you. Oh boy, our mural is looking fantastic, and this week we get to finish it! Let's see here. We have some things that remind us of the church, a bunch of question marks, and several number sevens. [*Challenge kids to recall Bible story details for each picture or symbol.*]

Today we are going to learn about something that is going to happen in the future: Jesus' return. Jesus promised that one day He will come back. What are some words that come to mind when you think about what that day will be like?

Choose a few volunteers to write words about Jesus' return anywhere on the large piece of paper. Encourage them to fill in empty white space to complete the mural.

Timeline map (1 minute)

- Timeline Map
- Bible Story Picture Poster (optional)

Leader •This is our last story on the timeline, but don't worry. This isn't the end of the story! It's about things that will happen in the future.

Point out today's Bible story picture on the timeline map, or if you framed and displayed the picture on wall, point it out for kids to see.

Leader •This is a picture of Jesus. Well, we don't really know exactly what Jesus looked like; they didn't have cameras in those days. But this is a picture that represents Jesus. Our Bible story is called "Jesus Christ Will Return." He *will*! What a wonderful promise!

Big picture question (1 minute)

Leader •You probably have a lot of questions about what will happen when Jesus returns. What will He look like? What will He be wearing? How will He return? Those are all questions we will talk about as we study the Bible story, but our big picture question today is, ***What will we do after Jesus returns?*** Let's find out.

Tell the Bible story (10 minutes)

- "Jesus Christ Will Return" video
- Bibles
- Bible Story Picture Slide or Poster
- Big Picture Question Slide or Poster

Open your Bible to Revelation 19 and tell the Bible story in your own words, or show the Bible story video "Jesus Christ Will Return."

Leader •When something is made known, that's called a *revelation*. The Book of Revelation is about the things God made known through John. In John's vision of heaven, John saw the things that would happen when Jesus comes back to earth.

Jesus will come riding on a white horse with His armies following behind Him. The name on His robe will be *King of kings and Lord of lords*. Jesus' enemies will be defeated and thrown into the lake of fire.

The Bible says that God will make a new heavens and a new earth. Everything God created in the beginning will be made new, the way God intended it to be before sin affected everything.

John saw this when he saw the Holy City, the new Jerusalem. The city came down from heaven. Its walls were made of jasper, and its gates were made of pearls. The street was pure gold, like clear glass.

John wrote that when Jesus returns, there will be no sadness, crying, or pain. Even though there will be no sun or moon for the new earth, there will be no darkness because the glory of God will be its light. And the Lord will reign forever and ever. What an amazing place heaven will be! *God will live with His people, and we will enjoy Him forever.*

Let's say our big picture question and answer together. *What will we do after Jesus returns? God will live with His people, and we will enjoy Him forever.*

God's new creation will be so beautiful—better than anything we could imagine. We will be with all of God's people from all nations and all time. We will have new bodies that are perfect—bodies that don't get sick or hurt. And the best part is that Jesus will be there. We wouldn't enjoy all the treasures in heaven if the greatest treasure wasn't there Himself.

The Gospel: God's Plan for Me (optional)

• Bible

Using Scripture and the guide provided, explain to boys and girls how to become a Christian. Tell kids how they can respond, and provide counselors to speak with each kid individually. Guide counselors to use open-ended questions to allow kids to determine the direction of the conversation.

Encourage boys and girls to ask their parents, small group leaders, or other adults any questions they may have about becoming a Christian.

Key passage (5 minutes)

• Key Passage Slide or Poster
• "Alpha Omega" song

Leader • Can anyone say our key passage from memory? Let's hear it! [*Allow kids to recite Revelation 22:12-13.*]

These verses come from our Bible story today. John heard Jesus say these words, and John wrote them down. John wrote down the things God showed him. The Book of Revelation tells us what will happen when Jesus returns.

Play "Alpha Omega" and invite kids to sing along.

Discussion starter video (5 minutes)

• "Unit 36 Session 4" discussion starter video

Leader • We don't know exactly what heaven will be like, but the Bible does give us quite a few details about heaven and what we will do when Jesus returns. Check out this video. Have you ever heard any of these ideas about heaven?

Show the "Unit 36 Session 4" video.

Leader • Some ideas about heaven are based on tradition instead of the Bible. The Bible doesn't say we will sit on clouds and play harps all the time. Heaven won't be boring. We will not be disappointed. ***What will we do after Jesus returns? God will live with His people, and we will enjoy Him forever.***

Remind kids that when Jesus returns, there will be a new creation—a new heavens and a new earth. Everything God created will be made new, and we will live there with God. (See Isa. 65:17; 66:22; Rev. 21:1.)

Sing (3 minutes)

• "Glorious Day" song

Leader • Oh, just the thought of spending forever and ever with Jesus makes me want to sing! We don't know exactly what that day will be like, but we will not be disappointed! Will you sing with me?

Sing together "O Glorious Day."

Prayer (2 minutes)

• sticky notes
• markers

Leader • Thanks for coming, everyone. Before you go to your small groups, let's pray. I am so thankful that God hears our prayers. God is good, and we can trust Him. Is there anything you would like to pray about?

Give each kid a sticky note and a marker. Instruct kids to write about or draw a picture of something they would like to pray for. When kids finish, invite them to post their sticky notes to the mural page. Then lead the group in a brief time of prayer or allow a couple of volunteers to pray.

Dismiss to small groups

The Gospel: God's Plan for Me

Ask kids if they have ever heard the word *gospel*. Clarify that the word *gospel* means "good news." It is the message about Christ, the kingdom of God, and salvation. Use the following guide to share the gospel with kids.

God rules. Explain to kids that the Bible tells us God created everything, and He is in charge of everything. Invite a volunteer to read Genesis 1:1 from the Bible. Read Revelation 4:11 or Colossians 1:16-17 aloud and explain what these verses mean.

We sinned. Tell kids that since the time of Adam and Eve, everyone has chosen to disobey God. (Romans 3:23) The Bible calls this sin. Because God is holy, God cannot be around sin. Sin separates us from God and deserves God's punishment of death. (Romans 6:23)

God provided. Choose a child to read John 3:16 aloud. Say that God sent His Son, Jesus, the perfect solution to our sin problem, to rescue us from the punishment we deserve. It's something we, as sinners, could never earn on our own. Jesus alone saves us. Read and explain Ephesians 2:8-9.

Jesus gives. Share with kids that Jesus lived a perfect life, died on the cross for our sins, and rose again. Because Jesus gave up His life for us, we can be welcomed into God's family for eternity. This is the best gift ever! Read Romans 5:8; 2 Corinthians 5:21; or 1 Peter 3:18.

We respond. Tell kids that they can respond to Jesus. Read Romans 10:9-10,13. Review these aspects of our response: Believe in your heart that Jesus alone saves you through what He's already done on the cross. Repent, turning from self and sin to Jesus. Tell God and others that your faith is in Jesus.

Offer to talk with any child who is interested in responding to Jesus.

Small Group LEADER

Session Title: Jesus Christ Will Return
Bible Passage: Revelation 19–22
Big Picture Question: What will we do after Jesus returns? God will live with His people, and we will enjoy Him forever.
Key Passage: Revelation 22:12-13
Unit Christ Connection: Jesus is making all things new.

Key passage activity (5 minutes)

- Key Passage Poster
- colored paper squares
- markers
- timer

Write each word of Revelation 22:12-13 on separate squares of colored paper. Mix up the squares and arrange them facedown on the floor or table.

Challenge kids to turn over all the squares and arrange the key passage in the correct order. When you say go, start the timer. Invite kids to play several times and see if they can beat their best time.

Say • Who said these words? (*Jesus*)
• Who wrote down these words? (*John*)
• *What will we do after Jesus returns? God will live with His people, and we will enjoy Him forever.*

Bible story review & Bible skills (10 minutes)

- Bibles, 1 per kid
- Small Group Visual Pack

Option: Retell or review the Bible story using the bolded text of the Bible story script.

Give each kid a Bible. Guide them to turn to the Book of Revelation. Ask kids where in the Bible they can find Revelation. (*the last book*) Instruct them to find chapter 19.

Explain that John wrote the Book of Revelation. He was on an island when God gave him a vision and told John to write down what he saw. The Book of Revelation tells about Jesus' final victory over Satan and about the reward that awaits for believers.

Ask the following review questions. If kids don't know

the answer, give the reference for them to find the answer in the Bible.

1. John heard a large crowd. What was the crowd doing? (*praising God and rejoicing, Rev. 19:1-3*)
2. What was the rider called? (*Faithful and True, Rev. 19:11*)
3. What name was on the rider's robe and thigh? (*Kings of kings and Lord of lords, Rev. 19:16*)
4. What happened to Satan? (*Satan was thrown into the lake of fire, Rev. 20:10*)
5. What new places did John see? (*a new heaven and a new earth, Rev. 21:1*)
6. Where did the loud voice say God would live? (*with humanity, with His people; Rev. 21:3*)
7. Why did the New Jerusalem not need a sun or moon? (*the glory of God gave light to the city, there is no darkness; Rev. 21:24-25*)
8. What did Jesus say about His return? (*"I am coming quickly," Rev. 22:12*)

Say • *What will we do after Jesus returns? God will live with His people, and we will enjoy Him forever.*

• Jesus promised to come back to earth soon. When He returns, those who trust in Jesus will be with Him and enjoy Him forever. God will undo every bad thing caused by sin—no more death, no more pain, no more tears. Jesus is making all things new.

If you choose to review with boys and girls how to become a Christian, explain that kids are welcome to speak with you or another teacher if they have questions.

• **God rules.** God created and is in charge of everything. (Gen. 1:1; Rev. 4:11; Col. 1:16-17)
• **We sinned.** Since Adam and Eve, everyone has chosen to disobey God. (Rom. 3:23; 6:23)
• **God provided.** God sent His Son, Jesus, to rescue

us from the punishment we deserve. (John 3:16; Eph. 2:8-9)

- **Jesus gives.** Jesus lived a perfect life, died on the cross for our sins, and rose again so we can be welcomed into God's family. (Rom. 5:8; 2 Cor. 5:21; 1 Pet. 3:18)
- **We respond.** Believe that Jesus alone saves you. Repent. Tell God that your faith is in Jesus. (Rom. 10:9-10,13)

Activity choice (10 minutes)

- cones
- paper
- marker
- timer (optional)
- tape

Option 1: Hidden words

Before small groups, write the following words on separate pieces of paper: *injury, fever, loneliness, fear, sadness.*

Tape each paper to the bottom of a cone. Scatter the cones around the room so the papers are hidden. Include several cones without papers underneath.

At your signal, kids should walk around the room and look at the bottom of each cone. When a player finds a hidden word, she should carry the cone to the front of the room and place it next to the wall. If the cone does not have a hidden word, the player should return it to its place. When kids collect all the hidden words, the game is over.

Turn over each collected cone and lead the kids to read the word together. Then ask them to raise their hands if they have ever experienced what is written on the paper.

Say • All of these things are things we might experience because the world is broken. Sin affects everything. The Bible says a day is coming when Jesus will return. He will fix every broken thing, and He will take away sin and sadness and all of these things.

• *What will we do after Jesus returns? God will live with His people, and we will enjoy Him forever.*

Option 2: World wonders collage

- travel magazines
- scissors
- paper
- glue sticks

Provide travel magazines and encourage kids to browse and cut out pictures of places they'd like to visit. Instruct them to glue pictures onto pieces of paper to make a collage.

As kids work, invite them to point out what is appealing about each location. Is it the climate? The colors? The plants and animals? Remind kids that God created all of these places; God created everything!

Say • When sin entered the world, all of creation was affected. People were separated from God. The Bible says that creation is imperfect because of sin. [*See Rom. 8:20-21.*] As beautiful as the places in these magazines look, they aren't the paradise that God intended.

• But Jesus is making all things new! The Book of Revelation says that when Jesus returns, there will be a new heavens and a new earth. Creation will be perfect! *What will we do after Jesus returns? God will live with His people, and we will enjoy Him forever.*

Journal and prayer (5 minutes)

- markers
- journals
- Bibles
- Journal Page, 1 per kid (enhanced CD)
- "Ultimate Timeline Review" activity page, 1 per kid

Distribute journal pages and markers. Encourage kids to design posters that say *Come, Lord Jesus!* Pray, asking Jesus to save our friends who do not know Jesus as Lord.

As time allows, lead kids to complete the activity page "Ultimate Timeline Review." Challenge the class to work in pairs or small groups to number the stories in the correct order. Then review the Bible stories together. Allow kids to share what they remember about each story. (*Old Testament: 1, 3, 5, 2, 4, 6; New Testament: 11, 9, 12, 7, 8, 10*)

Understanding the Basic Characteristics of Older Kids

In Luke 2:52 we read, "And Jesus increased in wisdom, and stature, and in favor with God and with people."

We know that Jesus was fully God and we also know that He was fully man. As a human we know that Jesus grew according to God's plan for humans. According to Luke 2:52 we see that Jesus grew mentally, physically, spiritually, socially and emotionally.

If Jesus grew according to God's plan for a boy (which He did) then we can assume that kids today will also grow in these five areas.

As Christian educators of children, understanding these characteristics will help us to create systems and learning opportunities that help children to be successful in learning about God and His plan for their lives.

At LifeWay Kids, we are committed to creating resources that undergird these basic characteristics. Below you will find shares general characteristics of specific aged kids.

While every child will not fit into these parameters, generally speaking, keeping these characteristics in mind will help you create successful environments for learning, growing, and understanding.

First and Second Graders

Spiritual

➤ Like learning from the Bible
➤ Are interested in God's wonders in nature
➤ Are making conclusions about God and regard Jesus as a friend
➤ Are learning right form wrong
➤ Can take some responsibility for own actions
➤ Understand truth and honesty

Social/Emotional

➤ Can be self-critical
➤ Evaluate own conduct based on the conduct of others
➤ May cry easily when scolded
➤ Are sensitive to what others

think, and want approval

- ➤ Use own experiences to understand others
- ➤ Fight with words and like to brag
- ➤ Need frequent reassurance
- ➤ May avoid new or difficult situations
- ➤ Are often talkative
- ➤ Need to succeed in challenging situations

> If Jesus grew according to God's plan for a boy (which He did) then we can assume that kids today will also grow in these five areas.

Mental

- ➤ Have a good memory
- ➤ Cannot think abstractly
- ➤ Can follow directions
- ➤ Enjoy reading and being read to
- ➤ Are creative and enjoy creative play
- ➤ Frequently ask teachers for help
- ➤ Want work to be perfect and are afraid to fail
- ➤ Can become deeply absorbed in activities
- ➤ Are beginning to understand money and the benefits of an allowance Want to be independent but do not want to make mistakes
- ➤ Like all kinds of games

Physical

- ➤ Are developing small muscles
- ➤ Are active using entire body
- ➤ Have difficulty sitting for long periods of time and may tire easily
- ➤ Like using hands
- ➤ Do not have well-developed eye-hand coordination

Third and Fourth Graders

Spiritual

- ➤ Ask serious questions about religion
- ➤ Are often beginning to feel the need for a Savior
- ➤ Are developing values
- ➤ Can be truthful and honest
- ➤ Are growing conscious of self and of sin
- ➤ Have difficulty making decisions
- ➤ Want to do things the right way and may feel ashamed when wrong
- ➤ Think in terms of right and wrong more than good and evil

Social/Emotional

- ➤ Need to let off steam and may

take out feelings on others

➤ Like peers of the same sex and dislike the opposite sex

➤ Are eager to please and want to be liked by peers and adults

➤ Are interested in own community and country

➤ Are beginning to feel that the group is as important as self

➤ Boys shout; girls giggle and whisper

➤ Are great talkers and need to be allowed to talk

➤ Change moods quickly

➤ Worship heroes

➤ Like to work with others

Mental

➤ Attention spans are lengthening

➤ Are able to be involved in experiences that deal with feelings and thinking

➤ Like to experiment and find out how things are made

➤ Vary with peers in reading ability

➤ Value money

➤ Accept carefully worded criticism

➤ Are beginning to think abstractly

➤ Are eager to learn

Physical

➤ Like to draw and sketch

➤ Have good eye-hand coordination

➤ May overdo it with physical activities and have trouble calming down

➤ Have slow, steady growth and good muscle control; girls usually developing more quickly than boys

Preteens

Spiritual

➤ Have concepts of love and trust

➤ Have formed concepts of personal worth

➤ Feel deeply about own experiences; can be sensitive to others

➤ Beginning to adopt a religious belief system of their own

➤ Are ready for spiritual answers and directions

➤ Are developing a conscience and a value system

➤ Can make many choices, but may not follow through on long-term commitments

Social/Emotional

➤ Are motivated most by own interest and think of self, using own experiences

➤ Are aware of sex roles; have

changing attitudes toward the opposite sex

➤ Can accept rules, organizations, responsibilities, and leader-follower roles

➤ Can operate comfortably within a group

➤ Have deep need for companionship and approval of peers

➤ Like to win and improve on achievements

➤ Like acceptance and encouragement; can become easily discouraged

➤ Recognize and appreciate individual differences

➤ Are ready for responsibilities and opportunities for self-direction

➤ Are easily influenced emotionally and can cope with some feelings

Mental

➤ Can distinguish between fact and fiction

➤ Are imaginative, creative, and curious

➤ Are capable of deep thoughts

➤ Are beginning to think abstractly

➤ Have developed basic reading and writing skills

➤ Can accept and work toward short-term goals

➤ Can cope with success and failure

➤ Can concentrate when interested

➤ Think quickly and memorize easily

➤ Can discern time and space relationships

➤ Can express ideas, understand cause and effect, solve problems, and plan

Physical

➤ Like to use abundant energy and physical skills

➤ Are approaching puberty; girls are usually ahead of boys

➤ Have good coordination and muscle skills

Bill Emeott has served as a Kids Ministry Specialist for LifeWay since 2003.

Seven Reasons Why Kids Must Memorize Scripture

If you know kids at all, you know that the average kid can memorize just about anything! Toddlers learn their ABCs, numbers, shapes, and a variety of silly songs. I even knew a two-year-old who could recite the names of the presidential cabinet!

Preschoolers can take it even further and read sight words, say the Pledge of Allegiance, and sing longer sillier songs!

Grade schoolers memorize the Gettysburg address, their multiplication tables, and plenty of lyrics from the radio.

So for the average kid, Scripture memory should be no sweat! For the most part, however, kids do not know much Scripture. We as parents and kids ministry leaders need to help them. Here are seven reasons why kids must memorize Scripture.

1. To know Christ.

Help kids develop a relationship with Jesus by leading them to the verses that tell them the truth. Start with John 3:16 or Romans 6:23.

2. To fight sin

Most of us know that as we get older, the choices of life present themselves, and temptation faces us at every turn. Help kids "hide God's Word in their hearts, so that they might not sin against [Him]" (Psalm 119:11).

3. To glorify God

Help kids understand that they were put on this earth to glorify God in all they do. That means fellowship with Him in prayer and obedience to Him in action. Scripture can help them give glory to God in all they do. (Psalm 86:12)

4. To feel safe

Kids struggle with fear often. The Bible is full of verses that remind them that God is close, and they do not have to be afraid. (Philippians 4:6)

5. To know they are loved

The Bible is God's love letter to us. Help kids understand that God loves them so much, and nothing can separate them from His love through Jesus. (Romans 8:38-39)

6. To love others

God uses children to show His love. If a child understands that she is to love God with all her heart and her neighbor as herself, what a vessel she can be to shine His light throughout the world! (Luke 10:27)

Scripture memory might sound optional, but indeed it is essential.

7. To persevere

Kids need to know that they will go through hard times in life. The Bible teaches us to press on in the faith, run the race and persevere. (Hebrews 12:1-2)

Our kids need spiritual ammo to get through their lives. The Bible, our "sword of the spirit," is what we *must* give them. Scripture memory might sound optional, but indeed it is essential to run the race—no matter how old you are!

Jana Magruder serves as the Director of Kids Ministry Publishing.

Speak as a Child

What does it mean to speak as a child, anyway? First, speaking like a child and acting like a child are two different things. Second, to do the first doesn't require doing the second. In fact, a sign of maturity is understanding and demonstrating the difference.

Several years ago I spent a day observing Bible study sessions at a kids camp. Most of the presentations were noisy, active, a little rambunctious, and led by highly engaging and energized leaders. Basically the sessions presented serious content in a kid-friendly way. Good stuff!

One session drastically stood out from the rest for one basic reason – transubstantiation. You're familiar with that term, right?

The leader allowed his well-intentioned passion to take priority over both the prescribed content and the needs of the kids. He had put aside childish things and felt his audience should as well. He failed to realize his audience spoke, thought, and reasoned like children because they were children. (1 Corinthians 13:11)

While I'm still a little fuzzy on the subject of transubstantiation, the session did start me on a journey to discover how best to teach kids. Here are a few things I have learned along the way:

➤ Search the Scripture passage and lesson content for words and concepts that are difficult to understand and might need to be explained.

➤ Use a variety of illustrations and visuals to refocus short attention spans.

➤ Don't be afraid to ask questions, but be ready to both affirm and deflect unexpected and inappropriate answers.

➤ Teach in bite-sized chunks. God didn't create the world in a single day, so we shouldn't try to teach everything we know about it in a single session.

➤ Make your point clearly and repeatedly. Don't shy away from repetition. That's how we learn!

➤ Willingly admit you personally do not understand everything.

Jerry Wooley is the VBS guy! He serves as the Vacation Bible School Specialist for LifeWay.